Ravit Sharma #20

SIDE STUDIES
PRESTWICK HOUSE, INC.

D0448022

A MIDSUMMER NIGHT'S DREAM

WILLIAM SHAKESPEARE

Shakespeare's text

on the left;

a modern rendering

on the right.

Prestwick House

P.O. Box 658 • Clayton, DE 19938
Tel: 1.800.932.4593
Web site: www.prestwickhouse.com

ISBN: 1-58049-514-1
Copyright ©2003 by Prestwick House, Inc.

Table of Contents

DRAMATIS PERSONAE

THESEUS, Duke of Athens
EGEUS, father to Hermia
LYSANDER, in love with Hermia
DEMETRIUS, in love with Hermia
PHILOSTRATE, Master of the Revels to Theseus
QUINCE, a carpenter
SNUG, a joiner
BOTTOM, a weaver
FLUTE, a bellows-mender
SNOUT, a tinker
STARVELING, a tailor

HIPPOLYTA, Queen of the Amazons, bethrothed to Theseus
HERMIA, daughter to Egeus, in love with Lysander
HELENA, in love with Demetrius

OBERON, King of the Fairies
TITANIA, Queen of the Fairies
PUCK, or ROBIN GOODFELLOW
PEASEBLOSSOM, fairy
COBWEB, fairy
MOTH, fairy
MUSTARDSEED, fairy

PROLOGUE, PYRAMUS, THISBE, WALL, MOONSHINE, LION are presented
by: QUINCE, BOTTOM, FLUTE, SNOUT, STARVELING, AND SNUG

Other Fairies attending their King and Queen
Attendants on Theseus and Hippolyta

ACT I

SCENE I Athens
The Palace of Theseus

[Enter Theseus, Hippolyta, Philostrate, and Attendants]

THESEUS: Now, fair Hippolyta, our nuptial hour
   Draws on apace; four happy days bring in
   Another moon; but, O, methinks, how slow
   This old moon wanes! She lingers my desires,
5   Like to a step-dame or a dowager,
   Long withering out a young man's revenue.

HIPPOLYTA: Four days will quickly steep themselves in night;
   Four nights will quickly dream away the time;
   And then the moon, like to a silver bow
10   New-bent in heaven, shall behold the night
   Of our solemnities.

THESEUS: Go, Philostrate,
   Stir up the Athenian youth to merriments;
   Awake the pert and nimble spirit of mirth;
15   Turn melancholy forth to funerals;
   The pale companion is not for our pomp.
           [Exit Philostrate]
   Hippolyta, I woo'd thee with my sword,
   And won thy love doing thee injuries;
   But I will wed thee in another key,
20   With pomp, with triumph, and with revelling.

[Enter Egeus, and his daughter Hermia, Lysander, and Demetrius]

ACT I

SCENE I Athens
The Palace of Theseus

[Enter Theseus, Hippolyta, Philostrate, and Attendants]

THESEUS. *Fair Hippolyta, our marriage hour draws nearer. We shall be wed in four happy days. But, oh, how slowly this old moon fades! She prolongs my wishes like an old woman withers a young man's fortune.*

HIPPOLYTA. *These four days will quickly be followed by night; four nights will quickly dream away the time. Then the moon, bent like a silver bow, will behold the night of our vows.*

THESEUS. *Go, Philostrate, stir all the young Athenians to festivities and wake the pert and nimble spirit of fun. Leave somber thoughts only for funerals—that pale companion is not for our ceremonies.*
> *[Exit Philostrate]*
Hippolyta, I wooed you with my sword and won your love by doing injury to you, but I will wed you in another key—with pomp, with triumph, and with merriment.

[Enter Egeus, and his daughter Hermia, Lysander, and Demetrius]

EGEUS: Happy be Theseus, our renowned duke!

THESEUS: Thanks, good Egeus; what's the news with thee?

EGEUS: Full of vexation come I, with complaint
Against my child, my daughter Hermia.
25   Stand forth, Demetrius. My noble lord,
This man hath my consent to marry her.
Stand forth, Lysander. And, my gracious duke,
This man hath bewitch'd the bosom of my child.
Thou, thou, Lysander, thou hast given her rhymes,
30   And interchanged love-tokens with my child;
Thou hast by moonlight at her window sung,
With feigning voice, verses of feigning love,
And stolen the impression of her fantasy
35   With bracelets of thy hair, rings, gawds, conceits,
Knacks, trifles, nosegays, sweetmeats, messengers
Of strong prevailment in unharden'd youth;
With cunning hast thou filch'd my daughter's heart;
Turn'd her obedience, which is due to me,
40   To stubborn harshness. And, my gracious duke,
Be it so she will not here before your Grace
Consent to marry with Demetrius,
I beg the ancient privilege of Athens:
As she is mine, I may dispose of her;
45   Which shall be either to this gentleman
Or to her death, according to our law
Immediately provided in that case.

THESEUS: What say you, Hermia? Be advis'd, fair maid.
To you your father should be as a god;
50   One that composed your beauties; yea, and one
To whom you are but as a form in wax,
By him imprinted, and within his power
To leave the figure, or disfigure it.
Demetrius is a worthy gentleman.

55 HERMIA: So is Lysander.

EGEUS. *Theseus, our renowned Duke, I wish you happiness!*

THESEUS. *Thanks, good Egeus; what's new with you?*

EGEUS. *I am full of problems with my child, my daughter Hermia. Come forward Demetrius. My noble lord, this man has my consent to marry her. Come forward Lysander. And, my gracious Duke, this man has stolen the heart of my child. You, Lysander, you have given her poems and exchanged tokens of love with my child; you have sung by moonlight at her window—with appropriate voice, verses of false love—and stolen the thoughts of her fantasy with bracelets of your hair, rings, toys, poems, trifles, flowers and food— all strong enticement for innocent youth. With cunning you stole my daughter's heart; turned her obedience, which is due me, to stubbornness. And, my gracious Duke, sorry to say, she will not now consent to marry Demetrius. I beg the ancient privilege of Athens: as she is mine, I may deal with her. Either she marries this gentleman, according to our law, she goes to her death.*

THESEUS. *What do you say, Hermia? Be advised, fair maiden. Your father should be like a god to you—one that formed your beauty; yes, and one to whom you are only a wax form, ready to be imprinted by him. It is within his power to leave you as you are or change you. This Demetrius is a worthy gentleman.*

HERMIA. *So is Lysander.*

THESEUS: In himself he is;
            But in this kind, wanting your father's voice,
            The other must be held the worthier.

HERMIA: I would my father look'd but with my eyes.

60 THESEUS: Rather your eyes must with his judgment look.

HERMIA: I do entreat your Grace to pardon me.
            I know not by what power I am made bold,
            Nor how it may concern my modesty,
            In such a presence here to plead my thoughts;
65   But I beseech your Grace that I may know
            The worst that may befall me in this case,
            If I refuse to wed Demetrius.

THESEUS: Either to die the death, or to abjure
            For ever the society of men.
70   Therefore, fair Hermia, question your desires,
            Know of your youth, examine well your blood,
            Whether, if you yield not to your father's choice,
            You can endure the livery of a nun,
            For aye to be shady cloister mew'd,
75   To live a barren sister all your life,
            Chanting faint hymns to the cold fruitless moon.
            Thrice-blessed they that master so their blood
            To undergo such maiden pilgrimage;
80   But earthlier happy is the rose distill'd
            Than that which, withering on the virgin thorn
            Grows, lives, and dies, in single blessedness.

HERMIA: So will I grow, so live, so die, my lord,
            Ere I will yield my virgin patent up
85   Unto his lordship, whose unwished yoke
            My soul consents not to give sovereignty.

THESEUS: Take time to pause; and by the next new moon—
            The sealing-day betwixt my love and me

THESEUS. *He certainly is; but, since he lacks your father's favor, Demetrius must be held to be worthier.*

HERMIA. *I wish my father could see Lysander as I do.*

THESEUS. *Instead, you should see things as he does.*

HERMIA. *I do plead for your Grace to pardon me. I do not know by what power I have become so bold, or how it may affect my modesty to plead my views here, but I beg your Grace that I might know the worst that could happen to me in this case if I refuse to wed Demetrius.*

THESEUS. *Either you will be put to death, or you will be forced to leave society forever. Therefore, fair Hermia, re-think your desires, question the impatience of your youth, examine your soul well. If you do not yield to your father's choice, can you endure the clothes of a nun and be happy while enclosed in a nunnery. You would never bear children, chanting faint hymns to the cold fruitless moon. Those who master their desires to undergo such a virginal experience are very blessed; but you could be happier here than those who grow, live, and die in that condition.*

HERMIA. *I will grow, live, and die a nun, my lord, before I will yield my virginity to Demetrius. My soul will not consent to be joined with him.*

THESEUS. *Take time to think. But by the next new moon—the day when my love and I will be married—upon that day either*

90 For everlasting bond of fellowship,—
Upon that day either prepare to die
For disobedience to your father's will,
Or else to wed Demetrius, as he would,
Or on Diana's altar to protest
For aye austerity and single life.

95 DEMETRIUS: Relent, sweet Hermia; and, Lysander, yield
Thy crazed title to my certain right.

LYSANDER: You have her father's love, Demetrius;
Let me have Hermia's; do you marry him.

EGEUS: Scornful Lysander! True, he hath my love;
100 And what is mine my love shall render him;
And she is mine; and all my right of her
I do estate unto Demetrius.

LYSANDER: I am, my lord, as well derived as he,
As well possess'd; my love is more than his;
105 My fortunes every way as fairly rank'd,
If not with vantage, as Demetrius';
And, which is more than all these boasts can be,
I am belov'd of beauteous Hermia.
Why should not I then prosecute my right?
110 Demetrius, I'll avouch it to his head,
Made love to Nedar's daughter, Helena,
And won her soul; and she, sweet lady, dotes,
Devoutly dotes, dotes in idolatry,
Upon this spotted and inconstant man.

115 THESEUS: I must confess that I have heard so much,
And with Demetrius thought to have spoke thereof;
But, being over-full of self-affairs,
My mind did lose it. But, Demetrius, come;
And come, Egeus; you shall go with me;
120 I have some private schooling for you both.
For you, fair Hermia, look you arm yourself

10

prepare to die for disobeying your father's will and marrying Demetrius, or expect to take the vow of chastity forever.

DEMETRIUS. *Relent, sweet Hermia and, Lysander, give up your flawed title to my assured claim.*

LYSANDER. *You have her father's love, Demetrius; let me have Hermia's. Marry him.*

EGEUS. *Yes, Lysander. It is true, that he has my love. What is mine is his and she is mine. All my rights to her I do give to Demetrius.*

LYSANDER. *I am, my lord, as well born as he, and worth as much. My love is greater than his; my fortunes are every way as great a sum. I have every advantage that Demetrius has. What is more, despite all of these boasts, I am certainly loved by beautiful Hermia. Why should not I then pursue my right? Demetrius—I'll say it to his face—made love to Nedar's daughter, Helena, and won her soul. That sweet lady overwhelmingly loves this flawed and imperfect man.*

THESEUS. *I must tell you that I have heard a lot, and I already spoke to Demetrius about it. But my mind is full of my own thoughts. Come, Demetrius, and come, Egeus. You shall go with me. I have some private words for you both. As for you, fair Hermia, look to fit your fantasies to your father's will or else the law of Athens will give you up to*

To fit your fancies to your father's will,
Or else the law of Athens yields you up—
Which by no means we may extenuate—
125   To death, or to a vow of single life.
Come, my Hippolyta; what cheer, my love?
Demetrius and Egeus, go along;
I must employ you in some business
Against our nuptial, and confer with you
130   Of something nearly that concerns yourselves.

EGEUS: With duty and desire we follow you.
                    [Exeunt all but Lysander and Hermia]

LYSANDER: How now, my love! Why is your cheek so pale?
How chance the roses there do fade so fast?

HERMIA: Belike for want of rain, which I could well
135   Beteem them from the tempest of my eyes.

LYSANDER: Ay me! for aught that I could ever read,
Could ever hear by tale or history,
The course of true love never did run smooth;
But, either it was different in blood—

140 HERMIA: O cross! too high to be enthrall'd to low.

LYSANDER: Or else misgraffed in respect of years—

HERMIA: O spite! too old to be engag'd to young.

LYSANDER: Or else it stood upon the choice of friends—

HERMIA: O hell! to choose love by another's eyes.

145 LYSANDER: Or, if there were a sympathy in choice,
War, death, or sickness, did lay siege to it,
Making it momentary as a sound,
Swift as a shadow, short as any dream,

death. We cannot change it—death or the nunnery. Come, my Hippolyta—what is happening, my love? Demetrius, and Egeus, come along; I must discuss some business about our wedding, and confer with you about something that concerns you directly.

EGEUS. With duty and pleasure we follow you.

[Exit all but Lysander and Hermia]

LYSANDER. Well, my love! Why are your cheeks so pale? How can your rosey blush fade so fast?

HERMIA. Probably for lack of rain, which I could well supply them from the storms in my eyes.

LYSANDER. Ah me! I've never heard in either story or history that the course of true love ever runs smoothly. Either it was different in the heart—

HERMIA. O problem! Too large to be settled easily.

LYSANDER. Or else fit poorly in respect to years—

HERMIA. O spite! Too old to be engaged to the young.

LYSANDER. Or else it stood upon the choice of relatives.

HERMIA. O hell! To choose love using another's eyes.

LYSANDER. Or, if we tried to be sympathetic, war, death, or sickness would lay siege to it; making it as momentary as

Brief as the lightning in the collied night
150   That, in a spleen, unfolds both heaven and earth,
And ere a man hath power to say 'Behold!'
The jaws of darkness do devour it up;
So quick bright things come to confusion.

HERMIA: If then true lovers have ever cross'd,
155   It stands as an edict in destiny.
Then let us teach our trial patience,
Because it is a customary cross,
As due to love as thoughts and dreams and sighs,
Wishes and tears, poor fancy's followers.

160 LYSANDER: A good persuasion; therefore, hear me, Hermia.
I have a widow aunt, a dowager
Of great revenue, and she hath no child:
From Athens is her house remote seven leagues;
And she respects me as her only son.
165   There, gentle Hermia, may I marry thee;
And to that place the sharp Athenian law
Cannot pursue us. If thou lovest me then,
Steal forth thy father's house tomorrow night;
And in the wood, a league without the town,
170   Where I did meet thee once with Helena
To do observance to a morn of May,
There will I stay for thee.

HERMIA: My good Lysander!
I swear to thee, by Cupid's strongest bow,
175   By his best arrow, with the golden head,
By the simplicity of Venus' doves,
By that which knitteth souls and prospers loves,
And by that fire which burn'd the Carthage Queen,
When the false Troyan under sail was seen,
180   By all the vows that ever men have broke,
In number more than ever women spoke,
In that same place thou hast appointed me,
Tomorrow truly will I meet with thee.

a sound, swift as a shadow, short as any dream, brief as the lightning in the cloudy night, which reveals heaven and earth and before anyone could say "behold!" the jaws of darkness quickly bring things to confusion.

HERMIA. *True lovers have ever been presented problems which stand like orders to their destiny. Let us be disciplined because it is a typical problem of love similar to thoughts, dreams, sighs, wishes and tears-the followers of love.*

LYSANDER. *A good idea. Therefore, hear me, Hermia. I have a widowed aunt, someone of great wealth who has no child. Her house is 20 miles from Athens and she loves me like her only son. There, gentle Hermia, I may marry you and in that place the sharp Athenian law cannot pursue us. If you love me go quietly from your father's house tomorrow night. In the woods, only three miles from town-where I did met you once with Helena to celebrate May Day-there I will wait for you.*

HERMIA. *My good Lysander! I swear to you by Cupid's strongest bow, by his best arrow with its golden head and by the simplicity of Venus' doves which connect souls and promotes love, and by that funeral fire which burned Carthage's Queen when the false Trojan sails were seen—by all the vows that men have broken or woman have spoken—in the same place where you said, tomorrow I will meet you.*

15

LYSANDER: Keep promise, love. Look, here comes Helena.

[Enter Helena]

185   HERMIA: God speed fair Helena! Whither away?

      HELENA: Call you me fair? That fair again unsay.
           Demetrius loves your fair. O happy fair!
           Your eyes are lode-stars and your tongue's sweet air
           More tuneable than lark to shepherd's ear,
190   When wheat is green, when hawthorn buds appear.
           Sickness is catching; O, were favor so,
           Yours would I catch, fair Hermia, ere I go!
           My ear should catch your voice, my eye your eye,
           My tongue should catch your tongue's sweet melody.
195   Were the world mine, Demetrius being bated,
           The rest I'd give to be to you translated.
           O, teach me how you look, and with what art
           You sway the motion of Demetrius' heart!

      HERMIA: I frown upon him, yet he loves me still.

200   HELENA: O that your frowns would teach my smiles such skill!

      HERMIA: I give him curses, yet he gives me love.

      HELENA: O that my prayers could such affection move!

      HERMIA: The more I hate, the more he follows me.

      HELENA: The more I love, the more he hateth me.

205   HERMIA: His folly, Helena, is no fault of mine.

      HELENA: None, but your beauty; would that fault were mine!

      HERMIA: Take comfort: he no more shall see my face;
           Lysander and myself will fly this place.

LYSANDER. *Keep that promise, love. Look, here comes Helena.*

[Enter Helena]

HERMIA. *God speed, fair Helena! Where are you going?*

HELENA. *Do you call me fair? Take it back. Demetrius loves your light complexion. Lucky to be so fair! Your eyes are like guiding stars and your tongue's sweet sound is more pleasant than the lark is to a shepherd's ear in springtime. That sickness is catching; O, I wish I could catch your beauty, fair Hermia, before I go! My ear should catch your voice, my eye your eye; my tongue should catch your tongue's sweet melody. Were the world mine except for Demetrius, the rest I'd give to you. O, teach me how you look, and how you are able to sway the emotion of Demetrius' heart!*

HERMIA. *I frown at him, yet he still loves me.*

HELENA. *O, that your frowns could teach my smiles such skill!*

HERMIA. *I curse him, yet he still gives me love.*

HELENA. *O that my prayers could create such affection!*

HERMIA. *The more I hate, the more he follows me.*

HELENA. *The more I love, the more he hates me.*

HERMIA. *His folly, Helena, is no fault of mine.*

HELENA. *None, but your beauty. I wish I had that fault!*

HERMIA. *Take comfort, he will no longer see my face; Lysander and*

Before the time I did Lysander see,
210   Seem'd Athens as a paradise to me.
O, then, what graces in my love do dwell,
That he hath turn'd a heaven unto a hell!

LYSANDER: Helen, to you our minds we will unfold:
Tomorrow night, when Phoebe doth behold
215   Her silver visage in the watery glass,
Decking with liquid pearl the bladed grass,
A time that lovers' flights doth still conceal,
Through Athens' gates have we devised to steal.

HERMIA: And in the wood, where often you and I
220   Upon faint primrose-beds were wont to lie,
Emptying our bosoms of their counsel sweet,
There my Lysander and myself shall meet;
And thence from Athens turn away our eyes,
To seek new friends and stranger companies.
225   Farewell, sweet playfellow; pray thou for us,
And good luck grant thee thy Demetrius!
Keep word, Lysander; we must starve our sight
From lovers' food till morrow deep midnight.

LYSANDER: I will, my Hermia. [Exit Hermia] Helena, adieu;
230   As you on him, Demetrius dote on you.
                                [Exit]

HELENA: How happy some o'er other some can be!
Through Athens I am thought as fair as she.
But what of that? Demetrius thinks not so;
He will not know what all but he do know.
235   And as he errs, doting on Hermia's eyes,
So I, admiring of his qualities.
Things base and vile, holding no quantity,
Love can transpose to form and dignity.
Love looks not with the eyes, but with the mind;
240   And therefore is wing'd Cupid painted blind.
Nor hath Love's mind of any judgment taste;

myself will be fleeing from here. Before I saw Lysander, Athens seemed like a paradise to me. It is strange that my love's powers have turned a heaven into a hell!

LYSANDER. *Helen, we will explain our plans to you. Tomorrow night, when it is very late and the grass is covered with dew, then we will flee from Athens.*

HERMIA. *And in the woods where we often would lie upon small flower beds emptying our hearts of their love, there Lysander and I shall meet. We will turn our eyes away from Athens to seek new friends and different company. Farewell, sweet friend, pray for us. Good luck with Demetrius! Keep your word, Lysander; we must stay apart until midnight tomorrow.*

LYSANDER. *I will, Hermia. [Exit Hermia] Helena, good-bye. I hope Demetrius longs for you as well.*

[Exit]

HELENA. *How happy that would be! Throughout Athens I am thought of as just as pretty. But what of that? Demetrius doesn't think so; he does not know what everyone else does. And even though he mistakenly loves Hermia, I admire his good qualities. While things can be common and hold no pure qualities, love can change them to ideal form; love does not look with eyes, but rather with the mind. That is why Cupid is painted as a blind spirit. Love's judgement is equally hasty. Therefore, Love is said to be a child because*

19

Wings and no eyes, figure unheedy haste;
And therefore is Love said to be a child,
Because in choice he is so oft beguiled.
245 As waggish boys in game themselves forswear,
So the boy Love is perjured everywhere;
For ere Demetrius look'd on Hermia's eyne,
He hail'd down oaths that he was only mine;
And when this hail some heat from Hermia felt,
250 So he dissolv'd, and showers of oaths did melt.
I will go tell him of fair Hermia's flight;
Then to the wood will he tomorrow night
Pursue her; and for this intelligence
If I have thanks, it is a dear expense.
255 But herein mean I to enrich my pain,
To have his sight thither and back again.

[Exit]

SCENE II. Athens
Quince's house

[Enter Quince, Snug, Bottom, Flute, Snout, and Starveling]

QUINCE: Is all our company here?

BOTTOM: You were best to call them generally, man by man,
according to the scrip.

QUINCE: Here is the scroll of every man's name, which is thought
fit, through all Athens, to play in our interlude before the
5 duke and the duchess on his wedding-day at night.

BOTTOM: First, good Peter Quince, say what the play treats on; then
read the names of the actors; and so grow to a point.

in it, he is so often tricked. Boys in their games often swear that Love is unkind. Before Demetrius looked on the eyes of Hermia he swore that he was only mine. When he felt some heat from Hermia, he melted and those beautiful oaths dissolved. I will go tell him that Hermia has fled. He will go to the wood tomorrow night and pursue her. If he thanks me it will be costly since I mean to have him return to me.

[Exit.]

SCENE II Athens.
Quince's house

[Enter Quince, Snug, Bottom Flute, Snout, and Starveling]

QUINCE. (Speaking to the group) Is all our company here?

BOTTOM. It is best to call them "generally", man by man, according to our list.

QUINCE. Here is the scroll of every man's name who is thought fit throughout all of Athens to act in our short play before the Duke and the Duchess on their wedding night.

BOTTOM. First, good Peter Quince, say what the play is about. Then, read the names of the actors; and so come to a finish.

QUINCE: Marry, our play is, The most lamentable comedy and most
cruel death of Pyramus and Thisbe.

10   BOTTOM: A very good piece of work, I assure you, and a merry.
Now, good Peter Quince, call forth your actors by the scroll.
Masters, spread yourselves.

QUINCE: Answer as I call you. Nick Bottom, the weaver.

BOTTOM: Ready. Name what part I am for, and proceed.

15   QUINCE: You, Nick Bottom, are set down for Pyramus.

BOTTOM: What is Pyramus? A lover, or a tyrant?

QUINCE: A lover, that kills himself most gallant for love.

BOTTOM: That will ask some tears in the true performing of it. If I
do it, let the audience look to their eyes; I will move storms;
I will condole in some measure. To the rest: yet my chief
20   humor is for a tyrant. I could play Ercles rarely, or a part to
tear a cat in, to make all split.

'The raging rocks
And shivering shocks
Shall break the locks
25   Of prison gates;
And Phibbus' car
Shall shine from far,
And make and mar
The foolish Fates.'

30   This was lofty! Now name the rest of the players. This is
Ercles' vein, a tyrant's vein: a lover is more condoling.

QUINCE. Well, our play is 'The most Lamentable Comedy and most Cruel Death of Pyramus and Thisbe.'

BOTTOM. A very good piece of work, I assure you, and a funny one. Now, good Peter Quince, call forth your actors by this list. Masters, spread yourselves about.

QUINCE. Answer as I call you. [Reads from list] Nick Bottom, the weaver.

BOTTOM. Ready. Name what part I will have, and proceed.

QUINCE. You, Nick Bottom, will have the part of Pyramus.

BOTTOM. What is Pyramus? A lover, or a tyrant?

QUINCE. A lover, who kills himself most gallantly for love.

BOTTOM. I will need some tears to perform it. If I do it, let the audience look after their eyes since I will move storms. I will be very pitiful. But still, my chief ability is playing a tyrant. I could play Hercules very well or a part to rage in or to make a great noise. [Speaking dramatically]
  'The raging rocks
  And shivering shocks
  Shall break the locks
    Of prison gates;
  And Phibbus' car
  Shall shine from far,
  And make and mar
    The foolish Fates.'

I was great! Now name the rest of the players. (Posing) This is Hercules' style, a tyrant's stance. A lover is sadder.

QUINCE: Francis Flute, the bellows-mender.

FLUTE: Here, Peter Quince.

QUINCE: Flute, you must take Thisbe on you.

35 FLUTE: What is Thisbe? A wandering knight?

QUINCE: It is the lady that Pyramus must love.

FLUTE: Nay, faith, let not me play a woman; I have a beard coming.

QUINCE: That's all one; you shall play it in a mask, and you may speak as small as you will.

40 BOTTOM: An I may hide my face, let me play Thisbe too. I'll speak in a monstrous little voice: 'Thisne, Thisne!' [Then speaking small] 'Ah Pyramus, my lover dear! Thy Thisbe dear, and lady dear!'

QUINCE: No, no, you must play Pyramus; and, Flute, you Thisbe.

45 BOTTOM: Well, proceed.

QUINCE: Robin Starveling, the tailor.

STARVELING: Here, Peter Quince.

QUINCE: Robin Starveling, you must play Thisbe's mother. Tom Snout, the tinker.

50 SNOUT: Here, Peter Quince.

QUINCE. *(Reads from list)* Francis Flute, the bellows-mender.

FLUTE. *Here, Peter Quince.*

QUINCE. *Flute, you must take the part of Thisbe.*

FLUTE. *What type of person is Thisbe? A knight?*

QUINCE. *Thisbe is the lady that Pyramus must love.*

FLUTE. *Wait, now, I cannot play a woman; I have a beard growing.*

QUINCE. *That's no problem; you shall play the part in a mask and you may speak as quietly as you can.*

BOTTOM. *If I may hide my face, let me play Thisbe, too. I'll speak in a monstrous little voice. 'Thisne, Thisne!' (Then speaking small) 'Ah Pyramus, my dear lover! I am your Thisbe dear, and lady dear!'*

QUINCE. *No, no, you must play Pyramus; and, Flute, you have the part of Thisbe.*

BOTTOM. *Well, proceed.*

QUINCE. *[Reads from list] Robin Starveling, the tailor.*

STARVELING. *Here, Peter Quince.*

QUINCE. *Robin Starveling, you must play Thisbe's mother. [Reads from list] Tom Snout, the tinker.*

SNOUT. *Here, Peter Quince.*

QUINCE: You, Pyramus' father; myself, Thisbe's father; Snug, the joiner, you, the lion's part. And, I hope, here is a play fitted.

SNUG: Have you the lion's part written? Pray you, if it be, give it me, for I am slow of study.

55 QUINCE: You may do it extempore, for it is nothing but roaring.

BOTTOM: Let me play the lion too. I will roar that I will do any man's heart good to hear me; I will roar, that I will make the duke say 'Let him roar again, let him roar again.'

QUINCE: An you should do it too terribly, you would fright the
60 duchess and the ladies, that they would shriek; and that were enough to hang us all.

ALL: That would hang us, every mother's son.

BOTTOM: I grant you, friends, if you should fright the ladies out of their wits, they would have no more discretion but to hang
65 us; but I will aggravate my voice so, that I will roar you as gently as any sucking dove; I will roar you an 'twere any nightingale.

QUINCE: You can play no part but Pyramus; for Pyramus is a sweet-faced man; a proper man, as one shall see in a summer's
70 day; a most lovely gentleman-like man; therefore you must needs play Pyramus.

BOTTOM: Well, I will undertake it. What beard were I best to play it in?

QUINCE: Why, what you will.

QUINCE. *You will be Pyramus' father. I will play Thisbe's father. (Reads from list) Snug, the joiner, you have the lion's part. And, I hope, here is a play properly fitted with actors.*

SNUG. *Have you written the lion's part already? If it is, please give it to me, for I am slow of study.*

QUINCE. *You may do it spontaneously, for it is nothing but roaring.*

BOTTOM. *Let me play the lion, too. I will roar so that it will do any man's heart good to hear me. I will roar so that I will make the Duke say 'Let him roar again; let him roar again.'*

QUINCE. *If you should do it too terribly, you would frighten the Duchess and the ladies. They would shriek and that would be enough to hang us all.*

ALL. *That would hang us, every mother's son.*

BOTTOM. *I grant you, friends, if I should frighten the ladies out of their minds they would have no choice but to hang us. But I could change my voice so that I could roar as gently as any dove. I could roar like any nightingale.*

QUINCE. *You can play no part except Pyramus, for Pyramus is a nice-looking man—a proper man as anyone could see on a summer's day; a most lovely gentleman-like man. Therefore, you must play Pyramus.*

BOTTOM. *Well, I will undertake it. What beard were I best to play it in?*

QUINCE. *Why, whatever you have.*

27

75 BOTTOM: I will discharge it in either your straw color beard, your
orange-tawny beard, your purple-in-grain beard, or your
French crown color beard, your perfect yellow.

QUINCE: Some of your French crowns have no hair at all, and then
you will play barefaced. But, masters, here are your parts;
and I am to entreat you, request you, and desire you, to
80 con them by tomorrow night; and meet me in the palace
wood, a mile without the town, by moonlight; there will we
rehearse; for if we meet in the city, we shall be dogg'd with
company, and our devices known. In the mean time I will
draw a bill of properties, such as our play wants. I pray you,
85 fail me not.

BOTTOM: We will meet; and there we may rehearse most obscenely
and courageously. Take pains; be perfect; adieu.

QUINCE: At the duke's oak we meet.

BOTTOM: Enough; hold, or cut bow-strings.

[Exeunt]

BOTTOM. *I will discharge it in either your straw-colored beard, your orange-tawny beard, your purple-dyed beard, or your perfect yellow—like on the French coins.*

QUINCE. *Some of your French crowns have no hair at all, so you will then play it bare-faced. But, masters, here are your parts. (Passing out parts) I am asking you, requesting you, and desiring you to memorize them by tomorrow night and meet me in the palace woods, a mile from the town. By moonlight we will rehearse; for if we meet in the city, we shall be surrounded with company, and our preparations found out. In the meantime, I will draw up a list of props which our play needs. I pray you, do not fail me.*

BOTTOM. *We will meet; and there we may rehearse most vulgarly and courageously. Take pains; be perfect; good-bye.*

QUINCE. *At the Duke's oak we shall meet.*

BOTTOM. *Enough; hold to our agreement or we will be ruined.*

[Exit]

ACT II

SCENE I
A wood near Athens

[Enter a Fairy at One door, and Puck at another.]

PUCK: How now, spirit! whither wander you?

FAIRY: Over hill, over dale,
      Thorough bush, thorough brier,
  Over park, over pale,
      Thorough flood, thorough fire,
  I do wander every where,
  Swifter than the moon's sphere;
  And I serve the fairy queen,
  To dew her orbs upon the green.
  The cowslips tall her pensioners be;
  In their gold coats spots you see;
  Those be rubies, fairy favors,
  In those freckles live their savors.
  I must go seek some dewdrops here,
  And hang a pearl in every cowslip's ear.
  Farewell, thou lob of spirits; I'll be gone.
  Our queen and all her elves come here anon.

PUCK: The king doth keep his revels here tonight;
  Take heed the queen come not within his sight;
  For Oberon is passing fell and wrath,
  Because that she as her attendant hath

ACT II

SCENE I
A wood near Athens

[Enter a Fairy at one door, and Puck at another]

PUCK. *How now, spirit! Where do you wander?*

FAIRY. *Over hill, over dale, through bush, through thistles, over park, over enclosure, through flood, through fire, I do wander everywhere, swifter than the moon's sphere; and I serve the Fairy Queen to dew her fairy rings on the common ground. The tall flowers are her gentlemen in their gold coats complete with fairy rubies and wonderful perfumes. I must go seek some dew-drops, and hang a pearl in every flower's ear. Farewell, you spirits; I'll be gone. Our Queen and all her elves come here at once.*

PUCK. *Tonight the King has parties here. Be careful the Queen does not come not within his sight. Oberon is angry because she has as her attendant, a lovely boy stolen from an Indian*

A lovely boy, stolen from an Indian king.
She never had so sweet a changeling;
And jealous Oberon would have the child
25   Knight of his train, to trace the forests wild;
But she perforce withholds the loved boy,
Crowns him with flowers, and makes him all her joy.
And now they never meet in grove or green,
By fountain clear, or spangled starlight sheen,
30   But they do square, that all their elves for fear
Creep into acorn cups and hide them there.

FAIRY: Either I mistake your shape and making quite,
Or else you are that shrewd and knavish sprite
Call'd Robin Goodfellow. Are not you he
35   That frights the maidens of the villagery,
Skim milk, and sometimes labor in the quern,
And bootless make the breathless housewife churn,
And sometime make the drink to bear no barm,
Mislead night-wanderers, laughing at their harm?
40   Those that Hobgoblin call you, and sweet Puck,
You do their work, and they shall have good luck.
Are not you he?

PUCK: Thou speakest aright:
I am that merry wanderer of the night.
45   I jest to Oberon, and make him smile,
When I a fat and bean-fed horse beguile,
Neighing in likeness of a filly foal;
And sometime lurk I in a gossip's bowl
In very likeness of a roasted crab,
50   And, when she drinks, against her lips I bob,
And on her withered dewlap pour the ale.
The wisest aunt, telling the saddest tale,
Sometime for three-foot stool mistaketh me;
Then slip I from her bum, down topples she,
55   And 'tailor' cries, and falls into a cough;
And then the whole quire hold their hips and laugh,
And waxen in their mirth, and neeze, and swear
A merrier hour was never wasted there.
But, room, fairy! here comes Oberon.

king. She never had such a fairy child and jealous Oberon would have that same child. But she physically withholds the loved child, crowns him with flowers, and makes him all her joy. Now they never meet in grove or green, by fountain clear, or spangled starlight unless they fight so much that all their elves creep into acorn cups and hide themselves in fear.

FAIRY. *Either I mistake your shape and likeness or else you are that playful and prankster called Robin Goodfellow. Are you not he who frightens the maidens of the village, skims milk, and sometimes sneaks into the churner and mischievously makes the housewife work forever. You sometimes make the drinks go flat, mislead those who walk at night, and laugh at their problems? Do you, sweet Puck, do the work of goblins while they get the reward? Are you not he?*

PUCK. *You speak correctly. I am that merry wanderer of the night. I humor Oberon and make him smile when I trick a fat male horse by sounding like a young female horse. Sometime I lurk in a gossip's bowl disguised as a roasted crab, and, when she drinks, I bump against her lips, and on her withered neck pours the ale. The wisest aunt, telling the saddest tale, sometime mistakes me for a three-foot stool. Then I slip from under her butt, she topples down, cries, and falls coughing! Then the whole group holds their hips and laughs, and enlarging their mirth, and sneezing, and swearing—a merrier hour was never passed so quickly! But give me room, fairy, here comes Oberon.*

60   FAIRY: And here my mistress. Would that he were gone!

[Enter Oberon at one door, with his train, and Titania, at another, with hers.]

OBERON: Ill met by moonlight, proud Titania.

TITANIA: What, jealous Oberon! Fairies, skip hence;
       I have forsworn his bed and company.

OBERON: Tarry, rash wanton; am not I thy lord?

65   TITANIA: Then I must be thy lady; but I know
       When thou hast stolen away from fairy land,
       And in the shape of Corin sat all day,
       Playing on pipes of corn, and versing love
       To amorous Phillida. Why art thou here,
70   Come from the farthest steep of India?
       But that, forsooth, the bouncing Amazon,
       Your buskin'd mistress and your warrior love,
       To Theseus must be wedded, and you come
       To give their bed joy and prosperity?

75   OBERON: How canst thou thus, for shame, Titania,
       Glance at my credit with Hippolyta,
       Knowing I know thy love to Theseus?
       Didst not thou lead him through the glimmering night
       From Perigouna, whom he ravished?
80   And make him with fair Aegle break his faith,
       With Ariadne and Antiopa?

TITANIA: These are the forgeries of jealousy;
       And never, since the middle summer's spring,
       Met we on hill, in dale, forest, or mead,
85   By paved fountain, or by rushy brook,
       Or in the beached margent of the sea,
       To dance our ringlets to the whistling wind,
       But with thy brawls thou hast disturb'd our sport.

FAIRY. *And here is my mistress. I wish that he were not here!*

[Enter Oberon at one door, with his train, and Titania, at another, with hers]

OBERON. *It's unpleasant to meet you by moonlight, proud Titania.*

TITANIA. *Oh, jealous Oberon! Fairies, skip away; I have given up his bed and his company.*

OBERON. *Stay, rash creature; am I not your lord?*

TITANIA. *Then I must be your lady. But I remember when you stole away from fairyland and in the shape of a shepherd sat all day playing on pipes of corn, and creating love poems to sexy Phillida. Why are you here; have you come from the farthest depths of India? Truly, the bouncing Amazon, your mistress and your warrior love, must be wedded to Theseus, and you have come to bless their bed with joy and prosperity?*

OBERON. *How can you torment me thus. For shame, Titania. Why hint at my relationship with Hippolyta when I know of your love for Theseus? Did you not lead him through the glimmering night from his lover Perigouna, and make him break his faith with fair Aegles and other women like Ariadne and Antiopa?*

TITANIA. *These are just the false signs of your jealousy. Not since the middle of summer have we on hill, in dale, forest, or meadow, by paved fountain, or by reed-lined brook, or on the edge of the sea, danced in circles to the whistling wind without your accusations disturbing our sport. Therefore, the winds have spoken to us in vain as if in revenge, and*

Therefore the winds, piping to us in vain,
90   As in revenge, have suck'd up from the sea
Contagious fogs; which, falling in the land,
Hath every pelting river made so proud
That they have overborne their continents.
The ox hath therefore stretch'd his yoke in vain,
95   The ploughman lost his sweat, and the green corn
Hath rotted ere his youth attain'd a beard;
The fold stands empty in the drowned field,
And crows are fatted with the murrion flock;
The nine men's morris is fill'd up with mud,
100   And the quaint mazes in the wanton green,
For lack of tread, are undistinguishable.
The human mortals want their winter here;
No night is now with hymn or carol blest;
Therefore the moon, the governess of floods,
105   Pale in her anger, washes all the air,
That rheumatic diseases do abound.
And thorough this distemperature we see
The seasons alter: hoary-headed frosts
Fall in the fresh lap of the crimson rose;
110   And on old Hiems' thin and icy crown
An odorous chaplet of sweet summer buds
Is, as in mockery, set. The spring, the summer,
The childing autumn, angry winter, change
Their wonted liveries; and the mazed world,
115   By their increase, now knows not which is which.
And this same progeny of evils comes
From our debate, from our dissension;
We are their parents and original.

OBERON: Do you amend it, then; it lies in you.
120   Why should Titania cross her Oberon?
I do but beg a little changeling boy,
To be my henchman.

TITANIA: Set your heart at rest;
The fairy land buys not the child of me.

have sucked up from the sea diseased fogs. These fogs, falling in the land, have filled every river so full that they have overflowed their banks. The ox has stretched against his yoke in vain, the farmer has labored for nothing, and the green corn has rotted before it finished growing. The pens stand empty in the flooded field, and crows grow fat by the dead flock. The dancers are slowed up by mud, and the quaint mazes in the fields grow indistinguishable for lack of walking. The human mortals do not spend their winter here; no night is now blessed with hymn or carol; the moon, the governess of floods, pale with anger, washes all the air so that diseases of the lungs abound. And through this discomfort we even see the seasons alter. White frosts fall on the fresh growth of the crimson rose; on old winter's thin and icy crown a smelly covering of sweet summer buds is placed as if in mockery. The spring, the summer; the plentiful autumn, the angry winter—all change their usual clothes; and the amazed world, now knows not which is which. And this same offspring of evil comes from our debate, from our fighting; we are its parents and origin.

OBERON. Do change it, then; it is all your doing. Why does Titania cross her Oberon? I only ask for a little boy to be my servant.

TITANIA. Give it a rest. All of fairyland cannot buy the child. His

125   His mother was a votaress of my order;
And, in the spiced Indian air, by night,
Full often hath she gossip'd by my side;
And sat with me on Neptune's yellow sands,
Marking the embarked traders on the flood;
130   When we have laugh'd to see the sails conceive,
And grow big-bellied with the wanton wind;
Which she, with pretty and with swimming gait
Following,—her womb then rich with my young squire,—
Would imitate, and sail upon the land,
135   To fetch me trifles, and return again,
As from a voyage, rich with merchandise.
But she, being mortal, of that boy did die;
And for her sake do I rear up her boy;
And for her sake I will not part with him.

140 OBERON: How long within this wood intend you stay?

TITANIA: Perchance till after Theseus' wedding-day.
If you will patiently dance in our round,
And see our moonlight revels, go with us;
If not, shun me, and I will spare your haunts.

145 OBERON: Give me that boy, and I will go with thee.

TITANIA: Not for thy fairy kingdom. Fairies, away.
We shall chide downright if I longer stay.
                 [Exit Titania with her train]

OBERON: Well, go thy way; thou shalt not from this grove
Till I torment thee for this injury.
150   My gentle Puck, come hither. Thou rememberest
Since once I sat upon a promontory,
And heard a mermaid, on a dolphin's back
Uttering such dulcet and harmonious breath,
That the rude sea grew civil at her song,
155   And certain stars shot madly from their spheres
To hear the sea-maid's music.

mother was a worshiper of my order; and, in the spiced Indian air, by night, often has she spoken by my side and sat with me on Neptune's yellow sands, watching the merchants sail on the water. We have laughed to see the sails fill and grow big-bellied with the spirited wind. She would imitate them with a swimming motion. After, her womb then rich with my young squire, she would sail upon the land to fetch me trifles, and return again as if from a voyage, rich with merchandise. But she, being mortal, died when that boy was born. It is for her sake that I do raise her boy; and for her sake I will not part with him.

OBERON. How long do you intend to stay within this wood?

TITANIA. Probably until after Theseus' wedding day. If you will patiently dance in our circle and see our moonlight revels, go with us. If not, ignore me, and I will leave your haunts.

OBERON. Give me that boy and I will go with you.

TITANIA. Not for your whole fairy kingdom. Fairies, go away. We shall fight if I stay longer.
                    [Exit Titania with her train]

OBERON. Well, do what you want but you shall not go from this grove until I torment you for this insult. My gentle Puck, come here. Do you remember when I once sat upon a cliff and heard a mermaid on a dolphin's back uttering such beautiful and harmonious sound that the rough sea grew calm at her song, and shooting stars fell wildly from their orbits to hear the seamaiden's music?

PUCK: I remember.

OBERON: That very time I saw, but thou couldst not,
                Flying between the cold moon and the earth
160   Cupid all arm'd; a certain aim he took
                At a fair vestal throned by the west,
                And loosed his love-shaft smartly from his bow,
                As it should pierce a hundred thousand hearts;
                But I might see young Cupid's fiery shaft
165   Quench'd in the chaste beams of the watery moon;
                And the imperial votaress passed on,
                In maiden meditation, fancy-free.
                Yet mark'd I where the bolt of Cupid fell.
                It fell upon a little western flower,
170   Before milk-white, now purple with love's wound,
                And maidens call it love-in-idleness.
                Fetch me that flower, the herb I shew'd thee once.
                The juice of it on sleeping eye-lids laid
                Will make or man or woman madly dote
175   Upon the next live creature that it sees.
                Fetch me this herb, and be thou here again
                Ere the leviathan can swim a league.

PUCK: I'll put a girdle round about the earth
                In forty minutes.
                                            [Exit Puck]

180
        OBERON: Having once this juice,
                I'll watch Titania when she is asleep,
                And drop the liquor of it in her eyes;
                The next thing then she waking looks upon,
                Be it on lion, bear, or wolf, or bull,
185   On meddling monkey, or on busy ape,
                She shall pursue it with the soul of love.
                And ere I take this charm from off her sight,
                As I can take it with another herb,
                I'll make her render up her page to me.
190   But who comes here? I am invisible;
                And I will overhear their conference.

Puck. *I remember.*

Oberon. *That time I saw, but you could not, flying between the cold moon and the earth, a well-armed cupid who took aim at a fair maiden throned in the west, and let his arrow fly as if to pierce a hundred thousand hearts. I saw young Cupid's fiery shaft quenched in the pure beams of the moon; and the imperial maiden passed on, in meditation, untouched. But I noted where the arrow from Cupid fell. It fell upon a little white western flower which became purple with love's wound. Maidens call it the pansy. Fetch me that flower. Drop the juice of it on sleeping eyelids and it will make man or woman madly love the next live creature that it sees. Fetch me this herb; return before the whale can swim a mile.*

Puck. *I'll circle the earth in forty minutes.*

[Exit Puck]

Oberon. *Having this juice, I'll watch Titania when she is asleep and drop the liquid into her eyes. The next thing then she looks on after waking, be it a lion, bear, wolf, bull, monkey, or ape, she shall then pursue with all her passion. Before I take this charm from her with another herb, I'll make her give up her boy to me. But who comes here? I am invisible so I will overhear their words.*

[Enter Demetrius, Helena following him.]

DEMETRIUS: I love thee not, therefore pursue me not.
　　　　　Where is Lysander and fair Hermia?
　　　　　The one I'll slay, the other slayeth me.
195　　　Thou told'st me they were stolen unto this wood,
　　　　　And here am I, and wode within this wood,
　　　　　Because I cannot meet my Hermia.
　　　　　Hence, get thee gone, and follow me no more.

HELENA: You draw me, you hard-hearted adamant;
200　　　But yet you draw not iron, for my heart
　　　　　Is true as steel. Leave you your power to draw,
　　　　　And I shall have no power to follow you.

DEMETRIUS: Do I entice you? Do I speak you fair?
　　　　　Or, rather, do I not in plainest truth
205　　　Tell you I do not nor I cannot love you?

HELENA: And even for that do I love you the more.
　　　　　I am your spaniel; and, Demetrius,
　　　　　The more you beat me, I will fawn on you.
　　　　　Use me but as your spaniel, spurn me, strike me,
210　　　Neglect me, lose me; only give me leave,
　　　　　Unworthy as I am, to follow you.
　　　　　What worser place can I beg in your love,—
　　　　　And yet a place of high respect with me,—
　　　　　Than to be used as you use your dog?

215　DEMETRIUS: Tempt not too much the hatred of my spirit;
　　　　　For I am sick when I do look on thee.

HELENA: And I am sick when I look not on you.

DEMETRIUS: You do impeach your modesty too much
　　　　　To leave the city and commit yourself
220　　　Into the hands of one that loves you not;
　　　　　To trust the opportunity of night,
　　　　　And the ill counsel of a desert place,
　　　　　With the rich worth of your virginity.

[Enter Demetrius, Helena following him.]

DEMETRIUS. *I do not love you. Therefore, do not pursue me. Where are Lysander and fair Hermia? The one I'll kill, the other kills me. You told me they sneaked into this wood. I am here, and feel wooden within this woods because I cannot meet my Hermia. Away. Go away, and follow me no more.*

HELENA. *You attract me, you stubborn man; but you do not draw iron for my heart is as true as steel. Rid yourself of your power to entice me and I shall have no need to follow you.*

DEMETRIUS. *How do I entice you? Do I speak nicely to you? Rather, do I not in plain words tell you that I do not nor I cannot love you?*

HELENA. *And, for that, I love you even more. I am your spaniel; and, Demetrius, the more you beat me, I will worship you. Use me as your dog. Neglect me, strike me, abuse me, lose me; only give me permission, unworthy as I am, to follow you. In what worse way could I beg for your love—and yet that a place is so highly respected by me—than to be used as you use your dog?*

DEMETRIUS. *Do not make me angry for I am sick when I do look at you.*

HELENA. *And I am sick when I do not look at you.*

DEMETRIUS. *You do harm your virtue too much to leave the city and commit yourself to the hands of one who does not love you, to trust the opportunity of night, and the ill counsel of a deserted place with the rich worth of your virginity.*

HELENA: Your virtue is my privilege for that:
225   It is not night when I do see your face,
        Therefore I think I am not in the night;
        Nor doth this wood lack worlds of company,
        For you, in my respect, are all the world.
        Then how can it be said I am alone
230   When all the world is here to look on me?

DEMETRIUS: I'll run from thee and hide me in the brakes,
        And leave thee to the mercy of wild beasts.

HELENA: The wildest hath not such a heart as you.
        Run when you will; the story shall be changed:
        Apollo flies, and Daphne holds the chase;
235   The dove pursues the griffin; the mild hind
        Makes speed to catch the tiger; bootless speed,
        When cowardice pursues and valour flies.

DEMETRIUS: I will not stay thy questions; let me go;
        Or, if thou follow me, do not believe
240   But I shall do thee mischief in the wood.

HELENA: Ay, in the temple, in the town, the field,
        You do me mischief. Fie, Demetrius!
        Your wrongs do set a scandal on my sex.
        We cannot fight for love as men may do;
245   We should be woo'd, and were not made to woo.
                     [Exit Demetrius]
        I'll follow thee, and make a heaven of hell,
        To die upon the hand I love so well.
                     [Exit Helena]

OBERON: Fare thee well, nymph; ere he do leave this grove,
        Thou shalt fly him, and he shall seek thy love.

[Re-enter Puck]

250   Hast thou the flower there? Welcome, wanderer.

HELENA. *Your virtue is my license to do that. It is not dark when I see your face; therefore, I think I am not in the night. Nor is this wood lacking company; for you, in my eyes, are all the world. How then can it be said I am alone when all the world is here to look at me?*

DEMETRIUS. *I'll run from you and hide in the woods, and leave you to the mercy of wild beasts.*

HELENA. *The wildest does not have a heart like yours. Run where you will; the legend shall be changed—Apollo flees, and Daphne chases; the dove pursues the lion; the mild deer runs to catch the tiger—fruitless speed when cowardice pursues and manliness flees.*

DEMETRIUS. *I will not listen; let me go. If you follow me, do believe that I shall do you wrong in the woods.*

HELENA. *Yes, in the temple, in the town, the field, you do me wrong. Shame Demetrius! Your wrongs make a woman do a scandalous act. We cannot fight for love as men may do; we should be won, and were not made to pursue others.*

> *[Exit Demetrius]*

I'll follow you, and make a heaven of this hell, to die upon the hand I love.

> *[Exit Helena]*

OBERON. *Farewell, nymph. Before he leaves this grove, you shall flee from him, and he shall seek your love.*

[Re-enter Puck]

PUCK: Ay, there it is.

OBERON: I pray thee give it me.
        I know a bank where the wild thyme blows,
        Where oxlips and the nodding violet grows,
255   Quite over-canopied with luscious woodbine,
        With sweet musk-roses, and with eglantine;
        There sleeps Titania sometime of the night,
        Lull'd in these flowers with dances and delight;
        And there the snake throws her enamell'd skin,
260   Weed wide enough to wrap a fairy in;
        And with the juice of this I'll streak her eyes,
        And make her full of hateful fantasies.
        Take thou some of it, and seek through this grove:
        A sweet Athenian lady is in love
265   With a disdainful youth; anoint his eyes;
        But do it when the next thing he espies
        May be the lady. Thou shalt know the man
        By the Athenian garments he hath on.
        Effect it with some care, that he may prove
270   More fond on her than she upon her love.
        And look thou meet me ere the first cock crow.

PUCK: Fear not, my lord; your servant shall do so.

                  [Exeunt]

Have you the flower there? Welcome, wanderer.

PUCK. Yes, here it is.

OBERON. Please give it to me. I know a river bank where the wild herb blows, where flowers and the nodding violet are covered over with luscious honeysuckle, with sweet large roses, and with small ones. There Titania sometimes sleeps, lulled in these flowers with dances and delights. There the snake throws off her jeweled skin, a cloth wide enough in which to wrap a fairy. With the juice of this I'll streak her eyes, and make her full of hateful fantasies. Take some of it and wander through this wood. A sweet Athenian lady is in love with a disdainful youth. Moisten his eyes so that the next thing he spies may be this lady. You shall know the man by the Athenian clothes he wears. Be careful so that he may prove more fond of her than she upon her love. Meet me before daybreak.

PUCK. Fear not, my lord. I shall do so.

[Exit]

SCENE II
Another part of the wood

[Enter Titania, with her train]

TITANIA: Come now, a roundel and a fairy song;
Then, for the third part of a minute, hence:
Some to kill cankers in the musk-rose buds;
Some war with rere-mice for their leathern wings,
5 To make my small elves coats; and some keep back
The clamorous owl that nightly hoots and wonders
At our quaint spirits. Sing me now asleep;
Then to your offices, and let me rest.

[The Fairies Sing]

FIRST FAIRY: [song]
10 You spotted snakes with double tongue,
Thorny hedgehogs, be not seen;
Newts and blind-worms, do no wrong,
Come not near our fairy Queen.

CHORUS
Philomel with melody
15 Sing in our sweet lullaby.
Lulla, lulla, lullaby; lulla, lulla, lullaby.
Never harm
Nor spell nor charm
Come our lovely lady nigh.
20 So good night, with lullaby.

SECOND FAIRY: Weaving spiders, come not here;
Hence, you long-legg'd spinners, hence.
Beetles black, approach not near;
Worm nor snail do no offence.

SCENE II
Another part of the wood

[Enter Titania, with her party]

TITANIA. [Speaking to the fairies] Quickly, come now, a dance and a fairy song. Shortly some will leave to kill worms in the rosebuds, some will fight with bats for their leathery wings. Others will fend off the owls. Sing me to sleep; then to your jobs, and let me rest.

[The Fairies Sing]

FIRST FAIRY. [Speaking to the bushes or ground] You spotted snakes with forked tongues, thorny hedgehogs, do not be seen here. Newts and lizards, do no wrong; do not come near our fairy Queen.

CHORUS.
Philomel, with melody now sings our sweet lullaby. (Sings) Lulla, lulla, lullaby; lulla, lulla, lullaby. Neither harm, nor spell, nor charm come near our lovely lady—so good night with a sweet lullaby.

SECOND FAIRY. Weaving spiders, do not come here. Away, you long-legged spinners, away! Black beetles, do not approach;

CHORUS

25   Philomel with melody, &c.

FIRST FAIRY: Hence away; now all is well.
          One aloof stand sentinel.

                    [Exeunt Fairies, Titania Sleeps]

[Enter Oberon and squeezes the flower on Titania's eyelids]

OBERON: What thou seest when thou dost wake,
          Do it for thy true-love take;
30   Love and languish for his sake.
          Be it ounce, or cat, or bear,
          Pard, or boar with bristled hair,
          In thy eye that shall appear
          When thou wakest, it is thy dear.
35   Wake when some vile thing is near.   [Exit]

[Enter Lysander and Hermia]

LYSANDER: Fair love, you faint with wandering in the wood;
          And, to speak troth, I have forgot our way;
          We'll rest us, Hermia, if you think it good,
          And tarry for the comfort of the day.

40 HERMIA: Be it so, Lysander: find you out a bed,
          For I upon this bank will rest my head.

LYSANDER: One turf shall serve as pillow for us both;
          One heart, one bed, two bosoms, and one troth.

45 HERMIA: Nay, good Lysander; for my sake, my dear,
          Lie further off yet; do not lie so near.

LYSANDER: O, take the sense, sweet, of my innocence!
          Love takes the meaning in love's conference.

worm or snail do no offense.

CHORUS.
   Philomel with melody, etc. [Titania Sleeps]

FIRST FAIRY. *Away from here; now all is well. One above us stands sentinel.*

[Exit Fairies]

[Enter Oberon and squeezes the flower on Titania's eyelids]

OBERON. *What you first see when you awake will you take for your true love; love and languish for his sake. Whether it is a lynx, a cat, a bear, a leopard, or boar with bristling hair— in your eye that shall seem most dear to you when you wake. Wake when some vile creature is near.*

[Exit]

[Enter Lysander and Hermia]

LYSANDER. *Fair love, you grow tired with this wandering and, to speak honestly, I have forgotten our way. We'll rest, Hermia, if you think it good, and wait for the sunrise.*

HERMIA. *Let it be so, Lysander. Find a bed, for I will rest my head upon this bank.*

LYSANDER. *One turf shall serve as pillow for both of us—one heart, one bed, two bosoms, and one truth.*

HERMIA. *No, good Lysander; for my sake, my dear, lie further off; do not lie so near to me.*

LYSANDER. *O, take the correct meaning, sweet, of my innocence!*

I mean, that my heart unto yours is knit,
So that but one heart we can make of it;
50 Two bosoms interchained with an oath,
So then two bosoms and a single troth.
Then by your side no bed-room me deny,
For lying so, Hermia, I do not lie.

HERMIA: Lysander riddles very prettily.
55 Now much beshrew my manners and my pride,
If Hermia meant to say Lysander lied!
But, gentle friend, for love and courtesy
Lie further off, in human modesty;
Such separation as may well be said
60 Becomes a virtuous bachelor and a maid,
So far be distant; and good night, sweet friend.
Thy love ne'er alter till thy sweet life end!

LYSANDER: Amen, amen, to that fair prayer say I;
And then end life when I end loyalty!
65 Here is my bed; sleep give thee all his rest!

HERMIA: With half that wish the wisher's eyes be press'd!
[They sleep]

[Enter Puck]

PUCK: Through the forest have I gone,
But Athenian found I none,
On whose eyes I might approve
70 This flower's force in stirring love.
Night and silence.—Who is here?
Weeds of Athens he doth wear:
This is he, my master said,
Despised the Athenian maid;
75 And here the maiden, sleeping sound,
On the dank and dirty ground.
Pretty soul! she durst not lie
Near this lack-love, this kill-courtesy.
Churl, upon thy eyes I throw

You should take the meaning of love's message. I mean that my heart is knit with yours so that only one heart can we make. Two bosoms connected with an oath, so then two bosoms and a single truth. Do not keep me from lying by your side. Lying thus, Hermia, I do not lie.

HERMIA. *Lysander riddles very smartly. I am ashamed of my manners and my pride to think to say Lysander lied! But, gentle friend, for love and courtesy lie further off because of human modesty. Such separation may well fit a virtuous bachelor and a maid. So be distant; and good night, sweet friend. Never alter your love until you die!*

LYSANDER. *Amen, amen, to that fair prayer. May my life be ended if I do not do it. Here is my bed; sleep give you rest!*

HERMIA. *I wish you can have the benefits of such sleep!*
        [They sleep]

[Enter Puck]

PUCK. *I have gone through the forest, but have found no Athenian on whose eyes I might place this flower's force of stirring love. Only night and silence—who comes here? Clothes from Athens he wears. This must be he who despised the Athenian maid. And here lies the maiden sleeping soundly on the wet and dirty ground. Pretty soul! She should not lie near this man who lacks love—this weak boy. Boy, upon your eyes I throw all the power this charm contains. When you wake let love consume you. Awake when I leave, for I must now go to Oberon.*

80   All the power this charm doth owe:
    When thou wakest let love forbid
    Sleep his seat on thy eyelid.
    So awake when I am gone;
    For I must now to Oberon. [Exit]

[Enter Demetrius and Helena, running]

85 HELENA: Stay, though thou kill me, sweet Demetrius.

  DEMETRIUS: I charge thee, hence, and do not haunt me thus.

  HELENA: O, wilt thou darkling leave me? Do not so.

  DEMETRIUS: Stay on thy peril; I alone will go.
                [Exit]

  HELENA: O, I am out of breath in this fond chase!
90   The more my prayer, the lesser is my grace.
    Happy is Hermia, wheresoe'er she lies,
    For she hath blessed and attractive eyes.
    How came her eyes so bright? Not with salt tears;
    If so, my eyes are oft'ner wash'd than hers.
95   No, no, I am as ugly as a bear,
    For beasts that meet me run away for fear;
    Therefore no marvel though Demetrius
    Do, as a monster, fly my presence thus.
    What wicked and dissembling glass of mine
100   Made me compare with Hermia's sphery eyne?
    But who is here? Lysander! on the ground!
    Dead, or asleep? I see no blood, no wound.
    Lysander, if you live, good sir, awake.

  LYSANDER: [Waking] And run through fire I will for thy sweet sake.
105   Transparent Helena! Nature shews art,
    That through thy bosom makes me see thy heart.
    Where is Demetrius? O, how fit a word
    Is that vile name to perish on my sword!

[Exit]

[Enter Demetrius and Helena, running]

HELENA. *Stop, though you kill me, sweet Demetrius.*

DEMETRIUS. *Please, leave and do not haunt me.*

HELENA. *O, will you leave me in this darkness? Do not do so.*

DEMETRIUS. *Stay at your own risk; I will go.*

[Exit]

HELENA. *O, I am out of breath in this chase! The more I ask, the less I receive from him. Hermia is happy wherever she lies for she has eyes which attract men. Why are her eyes so bright? She does not cry nearly as often as I do. No, no, I am as ugly as a bear. Beasts run away in fear when we meet. It is no wonder that Demetrius flies from me like I am a monster. Why has my wicked mirror forced me to compare myself with Hermia? (Seeing a sleeping figure) But who is this? Lysander! And on the ground! Is he dead, or asleep? I see no blood, no wound. Lysander, if you live, good sir, awake.*

LYSANDER. *[Waking] For your sweet sake I would run through fire. Oh, shining Helena! Nature shows the way to see your heart through your chest. Where is Demetrius? O, how*

HELENA: Do not say so, Lysander; say not so.
110   What though he love your Hermia? Lord, what though?
         Yet Hermia still loves you; then be content.

LYSANDER: Content with Hermia! No: I do repent
         The tedious minutes I with her have spent.
         Not Hermia but Helena I love:
115   Who will not change a raven for a dove?
         The will of man is by his reason sway'd,
         And reason says you are the worthier maid.
         Things growing are not ripe until their season;
         So I, being young, till now ripe not to reason;
120   And touching now the point of human skill,
         Reason becomes the marshal to my will,
         And leads me to your eyes, where I o'erlook
         Love's stories, written in Love's richest book.

HELENA: Wherefore was I to this keen mockery born?
125   When at your hands did I deserve this scorn?
         Is't not enough, is't not enough, young man,
         That I did never, no, nor never can,
         Deserve a sweet look from Demetrius' eye,
         But you must flout my insufficiency?
130   Good troth, you do me wrong, good sooth, you do,
         In such disdainful manner me to woo.
         But fare you well; perforce I must confess
         I thought you lord of more true gentleness.
         O, that a lady of one man refused
135   Should of another therefore be abused!

                                                [Exit]

LYSANDER: She sees not Hermia. Hermia, sleep thou there;
         And never mayst thou come Lysander near!
         For, as a surfeit of the sweetest things
         The deepest loathing to the stomach brings,
140   Or as the heresies that men do leave
         Are hated most of those they did deceive,

right it sounds to kill that name with my sword!

HELENA. *Do not say so, Lysander. Say it not so, even though he loves your Hermia. Lord, why does it matter if Hermia still loves you. Be content.*

LYSANDER. *Content with Hermia! No. I do repent the tedious minutes I spent with her. I love Helena, not Hermia. Who would not change junk for treasure? Man is swayed by his reason, and that reason says you are the worthier woman. Things only grow ripe over time; being so young I wasn't thinking straight until now. I now see your eyes filled with love.*

HELENA. *Why was I born for you to mock me? Do I deserve this scorn? Isn't it enough, young man, that I never did, nor never will, ever receive a sweet look from Demetrius. Do you have to make fun of my pain? Truly, you do me wrong—indeed, you do. Good-bye. But I must confess I thought you were a kinder man. O, that a lady who has been rejected by one man should be so abused by another!*

[Exit]

LYSANDER. *She does not see Hermia. Hermia, sleep there, and never come near to Lysander! The most hated lies of men are those in which we deceive. Others may hate my lies, but none more than me! Give me the strength to cherish Helen and be her love! And, all my powers, address your love and strength to honor Helen, and to be her knight!*

So thou, my surfeit and my heresy,
Of all be hated, but the most of me!
And, all my powers, address your love and might
145   To honor Helen, and to be her knight!
        [Exit]

Hermia: [Awaking] Help me, Lysander, help me; do thy best
        To pluck this crawling serpent from my breast.
        Ay me, for pity! What a dream was here!
150   Lysander, look how I do quake with fear.
        Methought a serpent eat my heart away,
        And you sat smiling at his cruel prey.
        Lysander! What, removed? Lysander! lord!
        What, out of hearing? gone? No sound, no word?
155   Alack, where are you? Speak, an if you hear;
        Speak, of all loves! I swoon almost with fear.
        No? Then I well perceive you are not nigh.
        Either death or you I'll find immediately.
                                              [Exit]

[Exit]

HERMIA. *[Starting] Help me, Lysander, help me! Do your best to pluck this crawling serpent from my breast. What a dream Lysander. Look how I do shiver with fear. I thought a serpent ate my heart and you sat by smiling. Lysander! What, gone? Lysander! Lord! What! Gone without a sound or a word? No sound, no word? Where are you? Speak, if you can hear me. Speak! I almost faint with fear. Not here? Not close by? Either death or you I'll find immediately.*

[Exit]

ACT III

SCENE 1

The wood. Titania lying asleep

[Enter Quince, Snug, Bottom, Flute, Snout, and Starveling]

BOTTOM: Are we all met?

QUINCE: Pat, pat; and here's a marvellous convenient place for our rehearsal. This green plot shall be our stage, this hawthorn-brake our tiring-house; and we will do it in action, as we will do it before the Duke.

5

BOTTOM: Peter Quince,—

QUINCE: What sayest thou, bully Bottom?

BOTTOM: There are things in this comedy of Pyramus and Thisbe that will never please. First, Pyramus must draw a sword to kill himself; which the ladies cannot abide. How answer you that?

10

SNOUT: By'r lakin, a parlous fear.

STARVELING: I believe we must leave the killing out, when all is done.

ACT III

SCENE I

The wood. Titania lying asleep

[Enter Quince, Snug, Bottom, Flute, Snout, and Starveling]

BOTTOM. Are we all here?

QUINCE. Yes, yes. Here's a marvelously convenient place for our rehearsal. This green spot shall be our stage, this group of trees our dressing room. We shall do a run through as if we were doing it before the Duke.

BOTTOM. Peter Quince!

QUINCE. What do you want, my friend?

BOTTOM. There are things in this comedy of Pyramus and Thisbe that are not pleasing. First, Pyramus must draw a sword to kill himself which the ladies will not tolerate. How do you answer that?

SNOUT. By our lady, a perilous fear.

STARVELING. I believe we must leave the killing out when all is said and done.

15 BOTTOM: Not a whit; I have a device to make all well. Write me
a prologue; and let the prologue seem to say we will do
no harm with our swords, and that Pyramus is not kill'd
indeed; and for the more better assurance, tell them that I
Pyramus am not Pyramus, but Bottom the weaver. This will
20 put them out of fear.

QUINCE: Well, we will have such a prologue; and it shall be written
in eight and six.

BOTTOM: No, make it two more; let it be written in eight and eight.

SNOUT: Will not the ladies be afeard of the lion?

25 STARVELING: I fear it, I promise you.

BOTTOM: Masters, you ought to consider with yourselves to bring
in—God shield us!—a lion among ladies is a most dreadful
thing; for there is not a more fearful wild-fowl than your
lion living; and we ought to look to't.

30 SNOUT: Therefore another prologue must tell he is not a lion.

BOTTOM: Nay, you must name his name, and half his face must be
seen through the lion's neck; and he himself must speak
through, saying thus, or to the same defect: —'Ladies,' —or
'Fair ladies,—I would wish you'—or 'I would request you'
35 —or 'I would entreat you,—not to fear, not to tremble. My
life for yours! If you think I come hither as a lion, it were
pity of my life. No, I am no such thing; I am a man as other
men are.' And there, indeed, let him name his name, and
tell them plainly he is Snug the joiner.

40 QUINCE: Well, it shall be so. But there is two hard things; that is,
to bring the moonlight into a chamber; for, you know,
Pyramus and Thisbe meet by moonlight.

BOTTOM. *Not a bit; I have a device to make it all well. Write me a prologue and let the prologue seem to say we will do no harm with our swords, and that Pyramus is not really killed; to be doubly sure, tell them that I am not Pyramus but rather Bottom the weaver. This will put them out of all fear.*

QUINCE. *Well, we will have such a prologue; and it shall be written in eight and six syllable lines.*

BOTTOM. *No, give it two more; let it be written in eight and eight.*

SNOUT. *Will not the ladies be afraid of the lion?*

STARVELING. *I fear it, I promise you.*

BOTTOM. *Masters, you ought to consider the fact—Heaven help us!—That a lion among ladies is a most dreadful thing. There is not a more dreadful animal than a lion—we ought to consider that.*

SNOUT. *Therefore another prologue must state that he is not really a lion.*

BOTTOM. *No, you must name his name, and half of his face must be seen through the costume. He himself must speak through the hole saying this, or something similar: 'Ladies,' or 'Fair ladies, I wish you' or 'I would request you' or 'I beg you not to fear, or tremble. My life will be laid down for yours! Do not think I come here as a lion. No, I am no such thing; I am a man as other men are.' And there, indeed, let him name the actor, and tell them plainly he is Snug the joiner.*

QUINCE. *It shall be so. But there are two hard problems to deal with. We must bring moonlight into the room, for, you know,*

63

SNOUT: Doth the moon shine that night we play our play?

45 BOTTOM: A calendar, a calendar! Look in the almanack; find out
moonshine, find out moonshine.

QUINCE: Yes, it doth shine that night.

BOTTOM: Why, then may you leave a casement of the great chamber
window, where we play, open; and the moon may shine in
50   at the casement.

QUINCE: Ay; or else one must come in with a bush of thorns and
a lantern, and say he comes to disfigure, or to present, the
person of moonshine. Then, there is another thing: we must
have a wall in the great chamber; for Pyramus and Thisbe,
55   says the story, did talk through the chink of a wall.

SNOUT: You can never bring in a wall. What say you, Bottom?

BOTTOM: Some man or other must present Wall; and let him have
some plaster, or some loam, or some rough-cast about
him, to signify wall; and let him hold his fingers thus, and
60   through that cranny shall Pyramus and Thisbe whisper.

QUINCE: If that may be, then all is well. Come, sit down, every
mother's son, and rehearse your parts. Pyramus, you begin;
when you have spoken your speech, enter into that brake;
and so every one according to his cue.

[Enter Puck behind]

Pyramus and Thisbe meet by moonlight.
SNOUT. *Does the moon shine the night we play our play?*

BOTTOM. *A calendar, a calendar! Look in the almanac; find out about moonshine, find out about moonshine.*

QUINCE. *Yes, it does shine that night.*

BOTTOM. *Why, then may you leave a panel of the great chamber window open where we play, and the moon may shine in at the opening.*

QUINCE. *Yes; or else one must come in with a bunch of sticks and a lantern. He will say that he comes representing the person of 'Moonshine'. Then there is another problem. We must have a wall in the great chamber since Pyramus and Thisbe, says the story, talked through a hole in a wall.*

SNOUT. *You can never bring in a wall. What do you say you, Bottom?*

BOTTOM. *Some man or other must represent 'Wall.' Let him have some plaster, or some dirt, or some building material with him to signify a wall. Let him hold his fingers like this [making a small circle with his fingers], and through that hole shall Pyramus and Thisbe whisper.*

QUINCE. *If that can be done, then all will be well. Come, sit down, every mother's son, and rehearse your parts. Pyramus, you may begin. When you have spoken your speech, go towards the woods; and so every one according to his cue.*

[Enter Puck behind]

65   PUCK: What hempen home-spuns have we swagg'ring here,
            So near the cradle of the fairy queen?
            What, a play toward! I'll be an auditor;
            An actor too perhaps, if I see cause.

  QUINCE: Speak, Pyramus. Thisbe, stand forth.

70   BOTTOM: Thisbe, the flowers of odious savors sweet—

  QUINCE: 'Odours,' odours!

  BOTTOM: —odours savors sweet;
            So hath thy breath, my dearest Thisbe dear.
            But hark, a voice! Stay thou but here awhile,
75   And by and by I will to thee appear.

                              [Exit]

  PUCK: A stranger Pyramus than e'er play'd here!

                              [Exit]

  FLUTE: Must I speak now?

  QUINCE: Ay, marry, must you; for you must understand he goes but
            to see a noise that he heard, and is to come again.

80   FLUTE: Most radiant Pyramus, most lily-white of hue,
            Of color like the red rose on triumphant brier,
            Most brisky juvenal, and eke most lovely Jew,
            As true as truest horse, that would never tire,
            I'll meet thee, Pyramus, at Ninny's tomb.

85   QUINCE: 'Ninus' tomb,' man! Why, you must not speak that yet;
            that you answer to Pyramus. You speak all your part at
            once, cues, and all. Pyramus enter: your cue is past; it is
            'never tire.'

  FLUTE: O— As true as truest horse, that yet would never tire.

PUCK. *What simple men do we have making noise here so near the bed of the Fairy Queen? What, a play! I'll be the judge; an actor, too, perhaps, if I see a need.*

QUINCE. *[Giving directions] Speak, Pyramus. Thisbe, stand here.*

BOTTOM. *Thisbe, the flowers of 'odious' smell so sweetly.*

QUINCE. *Not 'Odious'- odorous!*

BOTTOM. *—odors smell so sweetly; so does the breath of my dear Thisbe. But wait, a voice! Stay here a while, and by and by I will appear to you.*

[Exit]

PUCK. *A stranger Pyramus has never been played.*

[Exit]

FLUTE. *Should I speak now?*

QUINCE. *Yes, yes, you must; for you must understand he goes to see a noise that he heard and then comes back again.*

FLUTE. *Most beautiful Pyramus, most lily-white, of color like the red rose on a triumphant plant. Most frisky youth, and also most lovely outcast, as true as the truest horse who would never tire, I'll meet you, Pyramus, at Ninny's tomb.*

QUINCE. *'Ninus' tomb,' man! But, you must not speak that yet. That is your answer to Pyramus. You are speaking all your part at once, cues, and all. Pyramus enter. Your cue is already spoken; it was 'never tire.'*

67

[Re-enter Puck, and Bottom with an ass's head]

90 BOTTOM: If I were fair, Thisbe, I were only thine.

QUINCE: O monstrous! O strange! We are haunted. Pray, masters!
fly, masters! Help!

[Exeunt all but Bottom and Puck]

PUCK: I'll follow you; I'll lead you about a round,
Through bog, through bush, through brake, through brier;
95 Sometime a horse I'll be, sometime a hound,
A hog, a headless bear, sometime a fire;
And neigh, and bark, and grunt, and roar, and burn,
Like horse, hound, hog, bear, fire, at every turn.

[Exit]

BOTTOM: Why do they run away? This is a knavery of them to make
100 me afeard.

[Re-enter Snout]

SNOUT: O Bottom, thou art changed! What do I see on thee?

BOTTOM: What do you see? You see an ass-head of your own, do
you?

[Exit Snout]

[Re-enter Quince]

105 QUINCE: Bless thee, Bottom, bless thee! Thou art translated.

[Exit]

BOTTOM: I see their knavery: this is to make an ass of me; to fright
me, if they could. But I will not stir from this place, do what

FLUTE. [Repeating] O, as true as truest horse, that would never tire.
[Re-enter Puck, and Bottom with an ass's head]

BOTTOM. If I am gorgeous, Thisbe, I am yours.

QUINCE. (He sees Puck) O monster! O strangeness! We are haunted.
  Masters! Flee! Masters! Help!

[Exit all but Bottom and Puck]

PUCK. I'll follow you; I'll lead you about around through bog,
  through bush, through woods, through thorns. I'll sometimes be a horse, sometimes a hound, a hog, a headless
  bear, sometimes a fire. I'll neigh, and bark, and grunt, and
  roar, and burn, just like a horse, hound, hog, bear, fire.

[Exit]

BOTTOM. Why do they run away? Their stupid trick is to make me
  afraid.

[Re-enter Snout]

SNOUT. O Bottom, you are changed! What do I see on you?

BOTTOM. What do you see? You see your own ass-head!

[Exit Snout]

[Re-enter Quince]

QUINCE. Bless you, Bottom, bless you! You are changed.

[Exit]

BOTTOM. I see your silliness-you want to make an ass of me to

they can; I will walk up and down here, and will sing, that
they shall hear I am not afraid.   [Sings]

110   The ousel cock, so black of hue,
                      With orange-tawny bill,
               The throstle with his note so true,
                      The wren with little quill.

TITANIA: [Awakening] What angel wakes me from my flowery bed?

BOTTOM: [Sings]
115   The finch, the sparrow, and the lark,
                      The plain-song cuckoo gray,
               Whose note full many a man doth mark,
                      And dares not answer nay;—

120   for, indeed, who would set his wit to so foolish a bird? Who
         would give a bird the lie, though he cry 'cuckoo' never so?

TITANIA: I pray thee, gentle mortal, sing again.
           Mine ear is much enamored of thy note;
           So is mine eye enthralled to thy shape;
           And thy fair virtue's force perforce doth move me,
125   On the first view to say, to swear, I love thee.

BOTTOM: Methinks, mistress, you should have little reason for that.
          And yet, to say the truth, reason and love keep little compa-
          ny together now-a-days. The more the pity that some honest
          neighbors will not make them friends. Nay, I can gleek
130   upon occasion.

TITANIA: Thou art as wise as thou art beautiful.

BOTTOM: Not so, neither; but if I had wit enough to get out of this
          wood, I have enough to serve mine own turn.

TITANIA: Out of this wood do not desire to go;
135   Thou shalt remain here whether thou wilt or no.

frighten me if you can. But I will not leave this place. Do what they will; I will walk up and down here, and will sing so they will hear that I am not afraid. [Sings]

The blackbird, so black of hue, with orange-blonde beak, the thrush with his note so true, the wren with its little voice.

TITANIA. *What angel wakes me from my flowery bed?*

BOTTOM. [Sings]
The finch, the sparrow, and the lark, the plain song of the cuckoo whose full note many a man hears, and dares not answer. Indeed, who would link his voice to such a foolish bird? Who would call that bird a liar, even though he cries 'cuckoo'.

TITANIA. [Seeing Bottom] *Please gentle mortal, sing again. My ear is much   pleased by your song and my eye is enthralled by your shape. Your fair beauty moves me to say I love you. the first time I see you.*

BOTTOM. *I think, mistress, you should have little reason for that. And yet, to say truly, reason and love are seldom found together nowadays. It is a great pity that some honest neighbors will not make them friends. But, I am only kidding.*

TITANIA. *You are as wise as you are beautiful.*

BOTTOM. *Not so, neither. If I had enough sense to get out of this wood, I have enough to please myself.*

TITANIA. *Do not desire to go out of this wood. You shall remain here*

I am a spirit of no common rate;
The summer still doth tend upon my state;
And I do love thee; therefore, go with me.
I'll give thee fairies to attend on thee;
140   And they shall fetch thee jewels from the deep,
And sing, while thou on pressed flowers dost sleep;
And I will purge thy mortal grossness so
That thou shalt like an airy spirit go.
Peaseblossom! Cobweb! Moth! and Mustardseed!

[Enter Peaseblossom, Cobweb, Moth, and Mustardseed]

145   PEASEBLOSSOM: Ready.

COBWEB: And I.

MOTH: And I.

MUSTARDSEED: And I.

ALL: Where shall we go?

150   TITANIA: Be kind and courteous to this gentleman;
Hop in his walks, and gambol in his eyes;
Feed him with apricocks and dewberries,
With purple grapes, green figs, and mulberries;
The honey-bags steal from the humble-bees,
155   And for night-tapers crop their waxen thighs,
And light them at the fiery glow-worm's eyes,
To have my love to bed and to arise;
And pluck the wings from painted butterflies,
To fan the moonbeams from his sleeping eyes.
160   Nod to him, elves, and do him courtesies.

PEASEBLOSSOM: Hail, mortal!

COBWEB: Hail!

whether you want to or not. I am no common spirit. The summer still obeys my word. I do love you; therefore, go with me. I'll give you fairies to attend to you; and they shall fetch you jewels from the ocean, and sing while you lie on pressed flowers to sleep; and I will free your human body so you can move as a spirit does. Peaseblossom! Cobweb! Moth! Mustardseed!

[Enter Peaseblossom, Cobweb, Moth, and Mustardseed]

PEASEBLOSSOM. *Ready.*

COBWEB. *So am I.*

MOTH. *And I.*

MUSTARDSEED. *Me, too.*

ALL. *Where shall we go?*

TITANIA. *Be kind and courteous to this gentleman. Hop in his walks and play in his eyes; feed him with apricots and dewberries, with purple grapes, green figs, and mulberries. Steal honey bags from the bees, and for candles trim their wax legs, and snatch them from the fiery glow-worm's eyes. Have my love to bed and then arise. Pluck wings from the painted butterflies to fan the moonbeams from his sleeping eyes. Respect him, elves, and do him courtesies.*

PEASEBLOSSOM. *Hail, mortal!*

COBWEB. *Hail!*

MOTH: Hail!

MUSTARDSEED: Hail!

165 BOTTOM: I cry your worships mercy, heartily; I beseech your worship's name.

COBWEB: Cobweb.

BOTTOM: I shall desire you of more acquaintance, good Master Cobweb. If I cut my finger, I shall make bold with you.
170 Your name, honest gentleman?

PEASEBLOSSOM: Peaseblossom.

BOTTOM: I pray you, commend me to Mistress Squash, your mother, and to Master Peascod, your father. Good Master Peaseblossom, I shall desire you of more acquaintance too.
175 Your name, I beseech you, sir?

MUSTARDSEED: Mustardseed.

BOTTOM: Good Master Mustardseed, I know your patience well. That same cowardly giant-like ox-beef hath devoured many a gentleman of your house. I promise you your kindred
180 hath made my eyes water ere now. I desire your more acquaintance, good Master Mustardseed.

TITANIA: Come, wait upon him; lead him to my bower. The moon, methinks, looks with a watery eye; And when she weeps, weeps every little flower;
185 Lamenting some enforced chastity. Tie up my love's tongue, bring him silently.

[Exeunt]

Moth. *Hail!*

Mustardseed. *Hail!*

Bottom. *I cry for your worships' pardon. I ask your worship's name.*

Cobweb. *Cobweb.*

Bottom. *I shall desire to know more of you, good Master Cobweb. If I cut my finger, I shall have need of you. Your name, honest gentleman?*

Peaseblossom. *Peaseblossom.*

Bottom. *Please, commend me to Mistress Squash, your mother, and to Master Pea, your father. Good Master Peaseblossom, I shall desire to know you more too. Your name, please, sir?*

Mustardseed. *Mustardseed.*

Bottom. *Good Master Mustardseed, I know your patience well. Oxen have devoured many of your house. I promise you your kind has made my eyes water often. I desire to know you, good Master Mustardseed.*

Titania. *Come, wait upon him; lead him to my hiding spot. The moon, I think, looks with a watery eye; and when she weeps every little flower weeps for some violation of chastity. Tie up my love's tongue, bring him along silently.*

[Exit]

SCENE II

Another part of the wood

[Enter Oberon]

OBERON: I wonder if Titania be awaked;
    Then, what it was that next came in her eye,
    Which she must dote on in extremity.

[Enter Puck]

    Here comes my messenger.
5   How now, mad spirit!
    What night-rule now about this haunted grove?

PUCK: My mistress with a monster is in love.
    Near to her close and consecrated bower,
    While she was in her dull and sleeping hour,
10   A crew of patches, rude mechanicals,
    That work for bread upon Athenian stalls,
    Were met together to rehearse a play,
    Intended for great Theseus' nuptial-day.
    The shallowest thick-skin of that barren sort,
15   Who Pyramus presented, in their sport
    Forsook his scene and ent'red in a brake;
    When I did him at this advantage take,
    An ass's nole I fixed on his head.
    Anon his Thisbe must be answered,
20   And forth my mimic comes. When they him spy,
    As wild geese that the creeping fowler eye,
    Or russet-pated choughs, many in sort,
    Rising and cawing at the gun's report,
    Sever themselves and madly sweep the sky,
25   So, at his sight, away his fellows fly;
    And at our stamp here, o'er and o'er one falls;
    He murder cries, and help from Athens calls.

SCENE II

Another part of the wood

[Enter Oberon]

OBERON. I wonder if Titania is awake and what she saw then that she must dote on completely.

[Enter Puck]

Here comes my messenger. Well, mad spirit! What has happened in this haunted grove?

PUCK. My mistress is in love with a monster. A bunch of unsophisticated men were in the woods rehearsing a play for Theseus' wedding and came near her hiding spot while she slept. The dumbest of them was playing Pyramus. When he entered the wood, I took advantage of him and fixed a donkey's head on his. Soon his Thisbe called and I mimicked his answer. When they spied him, they fled madly as birds do when they hear guns go off, falling over each other in their panic. He cries murder and calls to Athens for help. Their senses were weak, lost within their fears, and many senseless acts began. Briers and thorns snatched at their apparel, catching some sleeves and some hats. I led them on in this distracted fear, and left donkey-headed Pyramus there. At that moment, Titania awoke, and straightway fell in love with an ass.

Their sense thus weak, lost with their fears thus strong,
Made senseless things begin to do them wrong,
30 For briers and thorns at their apparel snatch;
Some sleeves, some hats, from yielders all things catch.
I led them on in this distracted fear,
And left sweet Pyramus translated there;
When in that moment, so it came to pass,
35 Titania waked, and straightway loved an ass.

OBERON: This falls out better than I could devise.
But hast thou yet latch'd the Athenian's eyes
With the love-juice, as I did bid thee do?

PUCK: I took him sleeping,—that is finish'd too,—
40 And the Athenian woman by his side;
That, when he waked, of force she must be eyed.

[Enter Demetrius and Hermia]

OBERON: Stand close; this is the same Athenian.

PUCK: This is the woman, but not this the man.

DEMETRIUS: O, why rebuke you him that loves you so?
45 Lay breath so bitter on your bitter foe.

HERMIA: Now I but chide, but I should use thee worse,
For thou, I fear, hast given me cause to curse.
If thou hast slain Lysander in his sleep,
Being o'er shoes in blood, plunge in the deep,
50 And kill me too.
The sun was not so true unto the day
As he to me. Would he have stolen away
From sleeping Hermia? I'll believe as soon
This whole earth may be bored, and that the moon
55 May through the centre creep and so displease
Her brother's noontide with the Antipodes.
It cannot be but thou hast murder'd him;
So should a murderer look, so dead, so grim.

OBERON. *This is better than I could devise. But have you wetted the Athenian's eyes with the love-juice, as I bid?*

PUCK. *I did while he slept—all is finished and the Athenian woman is by his side so that, when he wakes, she will be seen immediately.*

[Enter Demetrius and Hermia]

OBERON. *Stand near; this is the same Athenian.*

PUCK. *This is the woman, but this is not the man.*

DEMETRIUS. *O, why do you rebuke he who loves you? Be bitter towards your bitter foe.*

HERMIA. [Angrily] *I'm not mad but I could be for, I fear, you have slain Lysander in his sleep. If you are his murderer, kill me, too. The sun is true to me. Would Lysander have left sleeping Hermia? I'll believe that as soon as this whole earth is cored through and the moon can be passed through it and ruin noon on the other side of the world. It cannot be other than you have murdered him. You have the murderer's look—so dead, so grim.*

DEMETRIUS: So should the murdered look; and so should I,
60   Pierced through the heart with your stern cruelty;
        Yet you, the murderer, look as bright, as clear,
        As yonder Venus in her glimmering sphere.

HERMIA: What's this to my Lysander? Where is he?
        Ah, good Demetrius, wilt thou give him me?

65   DEMETRIUS: I had rather give his carcass to my hounds.

HERMIA: Out, dog! out, cur! Thou drivest me past the bounds
        Of maiden's patience. Hast thou slain him, then?
        Henceforth be never number'd among men!
        O, once tell true; tell true, even for my sake!
70   Durst thou have look'd upon him being awake,
        And hast thou kill'd him sleeping? O brave touch!
        Could not a worm, an adder, do so much?
        An adder did it; for with doubler tongue
        Than thine, thou serpent, never adder stung.

75   DEMETRIUS: You spend your passion on a misprised mood:
        I am not guilty of Lysander's blood;
        Nor is he dead, for aught that I can tell.

HERMIA: I pray thee, tell me then that he is well.

DEMETRIUS: An if I could, what should I get therefore?

80   HERMIA: A privilege, never to see me more.
        And from thy hated presence part I so;
        See me no more whether, he be dead or no.

                    [Exit]

DEMETRIUS: There is no following her in this fierce vein;
        Here, therefore, for a while I will remain.
85   So sorrow's heaviness doth heavier grow
        For debt that bankrupt sleep doth sorrow owe;

DEMETRIUS. *So should the murdered person look, and so should I, pierced through the heart with your stern cruelty. Yet you, the murderer, look as bright, as clear, as Venus.*

HERMIA. *What's that to my Lysander? Where is he? Ah, good Demetrius, will you give him to me?*

DEMETRIUS. *I had rather give his carcass to my hounds.*

HERMIA. *Out, dog! Out, rat! You try my maiden's patience. Have you slain him, then? From now on be never numbered among men! O, at once tell the truth. Tell it true, for my sake! Did you look upon him awake and then killed him sleeping? [Sarcastically] O brave touch! Could not a snake, an adder, do as much? An adder did it, for with your forked tongue, you serpent, you have killed him.*

DEMETRIUS. *You spend your passion in the wrong direction. I am not guilty of Lysander's blood; nor is he dead as far as I know.*

HERMIA. *I pray you, tell me then that he is well.*

DEMETRIUS. *If I could, what should I get for it?*

HERMIA. *A privilege never to see me anymore. From your hated presence I will leave and you will see me no more whether he is dead or not.*

[Exit]

DEMETRIUS. *There is no following her in this fierce mood; here, therefore, I will remain for a while. Sorrow's heaviness*

Which now in some slight measure it will pay,
If for his tender here I make some stay.
           [Lies down and sleeps]

OBERON: What hast thou done? Thou hast mistaken quite,
90   And laid the love-juice on some true-love's sight.
Of thy misprision must perforce ensue
Some true love turn'd, and not a false turn'd true.

PUCK: Then fate o'er-rules, that, one man holding troth,
A million fail, confounding oath on oath.

95   OBERON: About the wood go swifter than the wind,
And Helena of Athens look thou find;
All fancy-sick she is and pale of cheer,
With sighs of love that costs the fresh blood dear.
By some illusion see thou bring her here;
100   I'll charm his eyes against she do appear.

PUCK: I go, I go; look how I go,
Swifter than arrow from the Tartar's bow.
                   [Exit]

OBERON: Flower of this purple dye,
Hit with Cupid's archery,
105   Sink in apple of his eye.
When his love he doth espy,
Let her shine as gloriously
As the Venus of the sky.
When thou wakest, if she be by,
110   Beg of her for remedy.

[Re-enter Puck]

PUCK: Captain of our fairy band,
Helena is here at hand,
And the youth, mistook by me
115   Pleading for a lover's fee;
Shall we their fond pageant see?
Lord, what fools these mortals be!

grows heavier with the debt that sleep owes. In some slight measure it will now pay, for I will rest here a while.
[Lies down]

OBERON. What have you done? You have made quite a mistake and placed the potion in the wrong eye. This was not what I had in mind with a true lover changed and the other not.

PUCK. Fate has overruled your plan.

OBERON. Go swifter than the wind, and find Helena of Athens. She is love struck and pale with sighs of love that costs her dearly. By some illusion see if you can bring her here; I'll try to charm his eyes against what she now does.

PUCK. I go, I go; look how I quickly go, swifter than an arrow.
[Exit]

OBERON. Flower of this purple dye, hit with Cupid's arrow and make her the apple of his eye. When his love he sees, let her shine as gloriously as Venus. When you wake, if she be near, beg remedy from her.

[Re-enter Puck]

PUCK. Captain of our fairies, Helena is here, and the youth mistaken by me is pleading for a lover's relief. Shall we see their meeting? Lord, what fools these mortals are!

OBERON: Stand aside. The noise they make
    Will cause Demetrius to awake.

PUCK: Then will two at once woo one.
120   That must needs be sport alone;
    And those things do best please me
    That befal preposterously.

[Enter Lysander and Helena]

LYSANDER: Why should you think that I should woo in scorn?
    Scorn and derision never come in tears.
125   Look when I vow, I weep; and vows so born,
    In their nativity all truth appears.
    How can these things in me seem scorn to you,
    Bearing the badge of faith, to prove them true?

HELENA: You do advance your cunning more and more.
130   When truth kills truth, O devilish-holy fray!
    These vows are Hermia's. Will you give her o'er?
    Weigh oath with oath, and you will nothing weigh:
    Your vows to her and me, put in two scales,
    Will even weigh; and both as light as tales.

135 LYSANDER: I had no judgment when to her I swore.

HELENA: Nor none, in my mind, now you give her o'er.

LYSANDER: Demetrius loves her, and he loves not you.

DEMETRIUS: [Awaking] O Helen, goddess, nymph, perfect, divine!
    To what, my love, shall I compare thine eyne?
140   Crystal is muddy. O, how ripe in show
    Thy lips, those kissing cherries, tempting grow!
    That pure congealed white, high Taurus' snow,
    Fann'd with the eastern wind, turns to a crow
    When thou hold'st up thy hand. O, let me kiss
145   This princess of pure white, this seal of bliss!

OBERON. *Stand aside. The noise they make will cause Demetrius to wake.*

PUCK. *Then will the two begin to court and this will be a rare sight. The stranger the scene, the better I'll like it.*

[Enter Lysander and Helena] .

LYSANDER. *Why do you think that I am teasing you? Scorn and derision never come with tears, and look, I weep. These new vows are all true. How can these true feelings in me seem scornful, bearing as they do my sincerest faith.*

HELENA. *[Angrily] You are even more tricky when truth kills truth. O what a tangled mess. These vows are for Hermia. Will you give her up? If we weigh pledge with pledge you will see no difference. Your vows to her and me, put on two scales, will weigh evenly and both are light and flimsy lies.*

LYSANDER. *I was not thinking when I swore to her.*

HELENA. *Nor are you now, when you give her up.*

LYSANDER. *Demetrius loves her, not you.*

DEMETRIUS. *[Awaking] O Helen, goddess, nymph, perfect, divine! To what, my love, shall I compare your eyes? Crystal is muddy. O, how ripe are your lips, those kissing cherries are very tempting! Pure snow looks dark when compared to your hand. O, let me kiss this princess of pure white, this seals our happiness! [Tries to kiss Helena]*

HELENA: O spite! O hell! I see you all are bent
                To set against me for your merriment.
                If you were civil and knew courtesy,
                You would not do me thus much injury.
150   Can you not hate me, as I know you do,
                But you must join in souls to mock me too?
                If you were men, as men you are in show,
                You would not use a gentle lady so:
                To vow, and swear, and superpraise my parts,
155   When I am sure you hate me with your hearts.
                You both are rivals, and love Hermia;
                And now both rivals, to mock Helena.
                A trim exploit, a manly enterprise,
                To conjure tears up in a poor maid's eyes
160   With your derision! None of noble sort
                Would so offend a virgin, and extort
                A poor soul's patience, all to make you sport.

LYSANDER: You are unkind, Demetrius; be not so;
                For you love Hermia. This you know I know;
165   And here, with all good will, with all my heart,
                In Hermia's love I yield you up my part;
                And yours of Helena to me bequeath,
                Whom I do love and will do till my death.

HELENA: Never did mockers waste more idle breath.

170 DEMETRIUS: Lysander, keep thy Hermia; I will none.
                If e'er I loved her, all that love is gone.
                My heart to her but as guest-wise sojourn'd,
                And now to Helen is it home return'd,
                There to remain.

175 LYSANDER: Helen, it is not so.

DEMETRIUS: Disparage not the faith thou dost not know,
                Lest, to thy peril, thou aby it dear.
                Look where thy love comes; yonder is thy dear.

HELENA. *O dog! O hell! I see you all of you are trying to have a joke at my expense. If you were civil and knew any kindness, you would not do me injury. Even if you hate me, do you have to mock me, too? If you were men as you act, you would not use a sweet lady like this. You pledge and swear, and praise me when I am sure you hate me indeed. You both are rivals and love Hermia, and now both rivals mock poor Helena. A real job, a manly enterprise to force tears to a poor maid's eyes with your scorn! None who are noble would so offend a virgin, and twist a poor soul's patience just to make sport.*

LYSANDER. *You are unkind, Demetrius; do not be so, for you love Hermia. This you know I know; and here, with all my good will, and with all my heart, I give to you my part in Hermia's love. Please give to me your love of Helena whom I do love and always will until death.*

HELENA. *Never did comedians ever have more idle breath.*

DEMETRIUS. *Lysander, keep Hermia; I will not do as you ask. If ever I loved her, all that love is now gone. My heart only traveled to her as a diversion and now it has returned home to Helen and will remain there.*

LYSANDER. *Helen, it can not be so.*

DEMETRIUS. *Don't belittle what you do not know since you might pay dearly for it.*

[Enter Hermia]

HERMIA: Dark night, that from the eye his function takes,
180   The ear more quick of apprehension makes;
    Wherein it doth impair the seeing sense,
    It pays the hearing double recompense.
    Thou art not by mine eye, Lysander, found;
    Mine ear, I thank it, brought me to thy sound.
185   But why unkindly didst thou leave me so?

LYSANDER: Why should he stay whom love doth press to go?

HERMIA: What love could press Lysander from my side?

LYSANDER: Lysander's love, that would not let him bide,
    Fair Helena, who more engilds the night
190   Than all yon fiery oes and eyes of light.
    Why seek'st thou me? Could not this make thee know,
    The hate I bare thee made me leave thee so?

HERMIA: You speak not as you think; it cannot be.

HELENA: Lo, she is one of this confederacy!
195   Now I perceive they have conjoin'd all three
    To fashion this false sport, in spite of me.
    Injurious Hermia! most ungrateful maid!
    Have you conspired, have you with these contrived,
    To bait me with this foul derision?
200   Is all the counsel that we two have shared,
    The sisters' vows, the hours that we have spent,
    When we have chid the hasty-footed time
    For parting us,—O, is all forgot?
    All school-days' friendship, childhood innocence?
205   We, Hermia, like two artificial gods,
    Have with our needles created both one flower,
    Both on one sampler, sitting on one cushion,
    Both warbling of one song, both in one key;
    As if our hands, our sides, voices, and minds,

[Enter Hermia]

HERMIA. Dark night keeps you from seeing clearly but it makes your hearing better. It impairs the seeing sense, but it pays the hearing one double. My eyes have not found Lysander but I hear him. [Finding Lysander] But why did you leave me?

LYSANDER. Why should he stay whom love forces to leave?

HERMIA. What love could force Lysander from my side?

LYSANDER. Lysander's love would not let him stay. It is fair Helena who makes the night shine more strongly than all the fiery stars and specks of light. Why do you seek me? Can you not figure out that my dislike for you made me leave you?

HERMIA. You do not speak as you feel—it cannot be.

HELENA. She is in on this conspiracy! Now I perceive that all three have joined to make this mean sport to spite me. Hurtful Hermia! Most ungrateful maiden! Have you conspired, have you joined with these two to tease me with this foul joke? Have all the secrets that we two have shared, the sisters' vows, the hours that we have spent together not wanting to leave each other—is this all forgotten? All our school-days' friendship, our childhood's innocence? We, Hermia, like two artificial gods, have knitted with our needles a single flower, whether it was by singing or talking or working together. Our hands, our sides, our voices, and our minds have been joined. We grew together like a double cherry, seemingly separate but still joined together. Two lovely berries molded on one stem with two bodies, but

210 Had been incorporate. So we grew together,
Like to a double cherry, seeming parted,
But yet an union in partition,
Two lovely berries moulded on one stem;
So, with two seeming bodies, but one heart;
215 Two of the first, like coats in heraldry,
Due but to one, and crowned with one crest.
And will you rent our ancient love asunder,
To join with men in scorning your poor friend?
It is not friendly, 'tis not maidenly;
220 Our sex, as well as I, may chide you for it,
Though I alone do feel the injury.

HERMIA: I am amazed at your passionate words;
I scorn you not; it seems that you scorn me.

HELENA: Have you not set Lysander, as in scorn,
225 To follow me and praise my eyes and face?
And made your other love, Demetrius,
Who even but now did spurn me with his foot,
To call me goddess, nymph, divine, and rare,
Precious, celestial? Wherefore speaks he this
230 To her he hates? And wherefore doth Lysander
Deny your love, so rich within his soul,
And tender me, forsooth, affection,
But by your setting on, by your consent?
What though I be not so in grace as you,
235 So hung upon with love, so fortunate,
But miserable most, to love unloved?
This you should pity rather than despise.

HERMIA: I understand not what you mean by this.

HELENA: Ay, do, persever, counterfeit sad looks,
240 Make mouths upon me when I turn my back,
Wink each at other; hold the sweet jest up;
This sport, well carried, shall be chronicled.
If you have any pity, grace, or manners,
You would not make me such an argument.
245 But fare ye well; 'tis partly my own fault,
Which death, or absence, soon shall remedy.

one heart, like a coat of arms belonging to a couple with a single crest. Will you tear our long love apart and join with scornful men to make fun of your poor friend? It is not friendly, nor maidenly. All females will be appalled that I feel this injury.

HERMIA. I am amazed at your passionate words; I do not hurt you; it seems that you hurt me.

HELENA. Didn't you set Lysander to follow me and praise my eyes and face to tease me? And did you not make your other love, Demetrius, who used to abuse me, call me goddess, nymph, goddess, rare, precious, and heavenly? Why does he speak these things now to one he hates? And why does Lysander deny he loves you, and fakes tenderness and affection for me except with your consent? Despite all of these romantic gestures from them, I am still miserable. You should pity rather than despise me.

HERMIA. I do not understand what you mean.

HELENA. You may fake sad looks and talk behind my back—carry this joke too far but it will be remembered. If you have style, or manners, you would not make fun at my expense. But good bye; it is partly my own fault which death, or leaving will soon remedy.

LYSANDER: Stay, gentle Helena; hear my excuse;
　　　　　My love, my life, my soul, fair Helena!

HELENA: O excellent!

250 HERMIA: Sweet, do not scorn her so.

DEMETRIUS: If she cannot entreat, I can compel.

LYSANDER: Thou canst compel no more than she entreat;
　　　　　Thy threats have no more strength than her weak prayers
255　　　　Helen, I love thee, by my life, I do;
　　　　　I swear by that which I will lose for thee
　　　　　To prove him false that says I love thee not.

DEMETRIUS: I say I love thee more than he can do.

LYSANDER: If thou say so, withdraw, and prove it too.

DEMETRIUS: Quick, come.

260 HERMIA: Lysander, whereto tends all this?

LYSANDER: Away, you Ethiope!

DEMETRIUS: No, no, he will
　　　　　Seem to break loose—take on as you would follow,
　　　　　But yet come not. You are a tame man; go!

265
LYSANDER: Hang off, thou cat, thou burr; vile thing, let loose,
　　　　　Or I will shake thee from me like a serpent.

HERMIA: Why are you grown so rude? What change is this,
　　　　　Sweet love?

270 LYSANDER: Thy love! Out, tawny Tartar, out!
　　　　　Out, loathed medicine! O hated potion, hence!

LYSANDER. *Stay, Helena; hear me out. My love, my life, my soul, fair Helena!*

HELENA. *O, great!*

HERMIA. *Sweet, do not scorn her so.*

DEMETRIUS. *If she cannot make you leave by her words, I can force you. I can compel you.*

LYSANDER. *You can force me only to the limit of her message. Your threats have no more strength than her weak prayers. Helena, I love you; with all my life I swear that I will die to disprove anyone who says I do not love you.*

DEMETRIUS. *I say I love you more than he does.*

LYSANDER. *If you say so, leave, and prove it that way!*

DEMETRIUS. *Quick, come.*

HERMIA. *Lysander, what is all this?*

LYSANDER. *Away, you outcast!*

DEMETRIUS. *No, no, he will break loose—come as if you would follow—but yet he comes not! You are a meek man; go!*

LYSANDER. *Let go, you cat, you burr; you vile thing, let loose or I will shake you from me like a serpent.*

HERMIA. *Why have you grown so rude? What change is this, sweet love?*

LYSANDER. *Your love! Out, brown barbarian, out! Out, hated*

HERMIA: Do you not jest?

HELENA: Yes, sooth; and so do you.

LYSANDER: Demetrius, I will keep my word with thee.

DEMETRIUS: I would I had your bond; for I perceive
275   A weak bond holds you; I'll not trust your word.

LYSANDER: What, should I hurt her, strike her, kill her dead?
        Although I hate her, I'll not harm her so.

HERMIA: What! Can you do me greater harm than hate?
        Hate me! wherefore? O me! what news, my love?
280   Am not I Hermia? Are not you Lysander?
        I am as fair now as I was erewhile.
        Since night you loved me; yet since night you left me.
        Why then, you left me,—O, the gods forbid!—
        In earnest, shall I say?

285   LYSANDER: Ay, by my life!
        And never did desire to see thee more.
        Therefore be out of hope, of question, of doubt;
        Be certain, nothing truer; 'tis no jest
        That I do hate thee and love Helena.

290   HERMIA: O me! you juggler! you cankerblossom!
        You thief of love! What! Have you come by night,
        And stolen my love's heart from him?

HELENA: Fine, i' faith!
        Have you no modesty, no maiden shame,
295   No touch of bashfulness? What! Will you tear
        Impatient answers from my gentle tongue?
        Fie, fie! you counterfeit, you puppet you!

medicine! O despised drink, away!

HERMIA. *Are you jesting?*

HELENA. *Yes, truly; and so do you.*

LYSANDER. *Demetrius, I will keep my word to you.*

DEMETRIUS. *I wish I had your bond; for I see a weak promise holding you; I'll not trust your word.*

LYSANDER. *What? Should I hurt her, strike her, kill her dead? Although I hate her, I'll not harm her.*

HERMIA. *What! Can you do me any greater harm than to hate me? Hate me! Why? O my! What news, my love? Am I not Hermia? Are you not Lysander? I am as fair now as I was before. During the night you loved me; yet during the night you left me. Why did you leave me. Heaven forbid!*

LYSANDER. *Aye, by my life! I never desire to see you again. Therefore, be out of hope, of question, of doubt. Be certain, nothing is truer. It is no joke that I hate you and love Helena.*

HERMIA. *O me! You two-timer! You worm! You thief of love! What! Have you come by night and stolen my love's heart from him?*

HELENA. *Indeed! Do you have no modesty, no shame? What! Will you tear impatient answers from my gentle tongue? Shame, shame! You imposter, you phony!*

HERMIA: 'Puppet!' why so? Ay, that way goes the game.
Now I perceive that she hath made compare
Between our statures; she hath urged her height;
300 And with her personage, her tall personage,
Her height, forsooth, she hath prevail'd with him.
And are you grown so high in his esteem
Because I am so dwarfish and so low?
How low am I, thou painted maypole? Speak.
305 How low am I? I am not yet so low
But that my nails can reach unto thine eyes.

HELENA: I pray you, though you mock me, gentlemen,
Let her not hurt me. I was never curst;
I have no gift at all in shrewishness;
310 I am a right maid for my cowardice;
Let her not strike me. You perhaps may think,
Because she is something lower than myself,
That I can match her.

HERMIA: 'Lower' hark, again.

315 HELENA: Good Hermia, do not be so bitter with me.
I evermore did love you, Hermia,
Did ever keep your counsels, never wrong'd you;
Save that, in love unto Demetrius,
I told him of your stealth unto this wood.
320 He followed you; for love I followed him;
But he hath chid me hence, and threatened me
To strike me, spurn me, nay, to kill me too;
And now, so you will let me quiet go,
To Athens will I bear my folly back,
325 And follow you no further. Let me go.
You see how simple and how fond I am.

HERMIA: Why, get you gone! Who is't that hinders you?

HELENA: A foolish heart that I leave here behind.

HERMIA. *Phony! Me? So that's your game. Now I see that you compare our heights. You have stood tall and with her figure—your tall figure—you have stolen his heart. You grow so high in his eyes because I am so short. How short am I, you painted maypole? Speak. How short am I? I am not yet so short that my nails cannot reach to your eyes.*

HELENA. *I beg you, even though you mock me, gentlemen, do not let her hurt me. I was never bad-tempered, I have no gift of meanness; but I am indeed afraid. Do not let her strike me. You perhaps may think because she is shorter than I am that I can be a match for her.*

HERMIA. *[Angrily] Again she says shorter!*

HELENA. *Good Hermia, do not be so bitter with me. I have always loved you, Hermia, kept your secrets, never wronged you. Even though I loved Demetrius, I told him of your trip to this wood. He followed you; for his love I followed. But he has yelled at me and threatened to strike me, leave me, and even to kill me. And now, if you will let me quietly go to Athens, I will return with my foolishness and follow you no further. Let me go. You see how simple I am and how fond I am of you.*

HERMIA. *Why, leave! Who is it who stops you?*

HELENA. *I leave my foolish heart there.*

HERMIA: What! with Lysander?

330   HELENA: With Demetrius.

LYSANDER: Be not afraid; she shall not harm thee, Helena.

DEMETRIUS: No, sir, she shall not, though you take her part.

HELENA: O, when she is angry, she is keen and shrewd;
        She was a vixen when she went to school;
335   And, though she be but little, she is fierce.

HERMIA: 'Little' again! Nothing but 'low' and 'little'!
        Why will you suffer her to flout me thus?
        Let me come to her.

LYSANDER: Get you gone, you dwarf;
340   You minimus, of hind'ring knot-grass made;
        You bead, you acorn.

DEMETRIUS: You are too officious
        In her behalf that scorns your services.
        Let her alone; speak not of Helena;
345   Take not her part; for if thou dost intend
        Never so little show of love to her,
        Thou shalt aby it.

LYSANDER: Now she holds me not.
        Now follow, if thou darest, to try whose right,
350   Of thine or mine, is most in Helena.

DEMETRIUS: Follow! Nay, I'll go with thee, cheek by jole.

                [Exeunt Lysander and Demetrius]

HERMIA: You, mistress, all this coil is 'long of you.
        Nay, go not back.

HERMIA. What! With Lysander?

HELENA. With Demetrius.

LYSANDER. Do not be afraid; she shall not harm you, Helena.

DEMETRIUS. No, sir, she shall not, even though you take her side.

HELENA. O, when she is angry, she is spirited; she was wild when she went to school; and, though she is little, she is fierce.

HERMIA. 'Little' again! Nothing but 'small' and 'little'! Why will you allow her to berate me like this? Let me at her.

LYSANDER. Get away, you dwarf. You little thing made from grass that stunts——you tiny bead, you acorn.

DEMETRIUS. You are too meddling in behalf of one who scorns your services. Leave her alone; speak not of Helena; do not take her part. If you intend to show a little love to her, you will pay for it.

LYSANDER. She does not hold me. Follow, if you dare, to determine who is most favored by Helena, you or I.

...s. Follow! No, I'll go with you, at your side as an equal.

[Exit Lysander and Demetrius]

HERMIA. Well, girl, all of this disruption is because of you.

HELENA: I will not trust you, I;
355   Nor longer stay in your curst company.
            Your hands than mine are quicker for a fray;
            My legs are longer though, to run away.   [Exit]

HERMIA: I am amazed, and know not what to say.   [Exit]

OBERON: This is thy negligence. Still thou mistakest,
360   Or else committ'st thy knaveries wilfully.

PUCK: Believe me, king of shadows, I mistook.
            Did not you tell me I should know the man
            By the Athenian garments he had on?
            And so far blameless proves my enterprise,
365   That I have 'nointed an Athenian's eyes;
            And so far am I glad it so did sort,
            As this their jangling I esteem a sport.

OBERON: Thou seest these lovers seek a place to fight.
            Hie therefore, Robin, overcast the night;
370   The starry welkin cover thou anon
            With drooping fog as black as Acheron,
            And lead these testy rivals so astray
            As one come not within another's way.
            Like to Lysander sometime frame thy tongue,
375   Then stir Demetrius up with bitter wrong;
            And sometime rail thou like Demetrius;
            And from each other look thou lead them thus,
            Till o'er their brows death-counterfeiting sleep
            With leaden legs and batty wings doth creep.
380   Then crush this herb into Lysander's eye;
            Whose liquor hath this virtuous property,
            To take from thence all error with his might
            And make his eyeballs roll with wonted sight.
            When they next wake, all this derision
385   Shall seem a dream and fruitless vision;
            And back to Athens shall the lovers wend,
            With league whose date till death shall neve̶
            Whiles I in this affair do thee employ,
            I'll to my queen, and beg her Indian b̶oy͗
390   And then I will her charmed eye rel̶ ̶ase
            From monster's view, and all thing̶ shall be peace.

100

HELENA. I will not trust you; I, will no longer stay in your cursed company. Your hands are better than mine in a fight but my legs are longer to run away.

[Exit]

HERMIA. I am amazed, and do not know what to say.

[Exit]

OBERON. This is your fault. You made mistakes or else did this on purpose.

PUCK. Believe me, king of shadows, I only made a mistake. Did you not tell me that I should know the man by his Athenian clothes. I am blameless in my job since I have anointed an Athenian's eyes. So far, I am glad it is working out so well since this misunderstanding seems a sport.

OBERON. You see how these lovers seek a place to fight. Go Robin. Make the night cloudy. Cover the stars with drooping fog as black as Hades, and lead these testy rivals apart so not one comes within the other's way. Sometimes frame your voice to sound like Lysander and tease Demetrius to follow you through the woods. Sometime sound like Demetrius to have Lysander chase you. Lead each away until sleep creeps upon them. Then crush this herb into Lysander's eye, whose strong liquid can set our problem straight. When they next awake, all of this problem will only seem like a dream. Back to Athens shall these lovers go and never part from each other. While you are doing this for me, I'll go to my queen and beg for her Indian boy. Then I will release her from the potion and all things shall be at peace.

PUCK: My fairy lord, this must be done with haste,
For night's swift dragons cut the clouds full fast;
And yonder shines Aurora's harbinger,
At whose approach, ghosts, wandering here and there,
395 Troop home to churchyards. Damned spirits all
That in crossways and floods have burial,
Already to their wormy beds are gone,
For fear lest day should look their shames upon;
They wilfully themselves exile from light,
400 And must for aye consort with black-brow'd night.

OBERON: But we are spirits of another sort:
I with the morning's love have oft made sport;
And, like a forester, the groves may tread
Even till the eastern gate, all fiery-red,
405 Opening on Neptune with fair blessed beams,
Turns into yellow gold his salt green streams.
But, notwithstanding, haste, make no delay;
We may effect this business yet ere day.

[Exit Oberon]

PUCK: Up and down, up and down,
410 I will lead them up and down.
I am fear'd in field and town.
Goblin, lead them up and down.
Here comes one.

[Enter Lysander]

415 LYSANDER: Where art thou, proud Demetrius? Speak thou now.

PUCK: Here, villain, drawn and ready. Where art thou?

LYSANDER: I will be with thee straight.

PUCK: Follow me, then,
To plainer ground.

[Exit Lysander as following the voice]

PUCK. My fairy lord, this must be done quickly since the clouds are disappearing and the morning star appears. Wandering spirits troop home to church-yards. Damned spirits who are buried at crossroads have already gone to their wormy beds before daylight would see their shame. They hide from the approaching day.

OBERON. But we are spirits of another sort. I have often loved the dawn with its fiery red color and walked like a forester in the woods.

[Exit Oberon]

PUCK. Up and down, up and down, I will lead them up and down. I am feared in field and town. Goblin, lead them up and down. Here comes one.

[Enter Lysander]

LYSANDER. Where are you, Demetrius? Speak now.

PUCK. [Sounding like Demetrius] Here, villain, with sword drawn and ready. Where are you?

LYSANDER. I will be with you immediately.

PUCK. Follow me, then, to level ground.

[Enter Demetrius]

420   DEMETRIUS: Lysander, speak again.
          Thou runaway, thou coward, art thou fled?
          Speak! In some bush? Where dost thou hide thy head?

  PUCK: Thou coward, art thou bragging to the stars,
          Telling the bushes that thou look'st for wars,
425   And wilt not come? Come, recreant, come, thou child;
          I'll whip thee with a rod. He is defiled
          That draws a sword on thee.

  DEMETRIUS: Yea, art thou there?

  PUCK: Follow my voice; we'll try no manhood here.

                           [Exeunt]

[Re-enter Lysander]

430   LYSANDER: He goes before me, and still dares me on;
          When I come where he calls, then he is gone.
          The villain is much lighter-heel'd than I.
          I followed fast, but faster he did fly,
          That fallen am I in dark uneven way,
435   And here will rest me. [Lies down] Come, thou gentle day.
          For if but once thou show me thy grey light,
          I'll find Demetrius, and revenge this spite.

                          [Sleeps]

[Re-enter Puck and Demetrius]

  PUCK: Ho, ho, ho! Coward, why com'st thou not?

  DEMETRIUS: Abide me, if thou darest; for well I wot
440   Thou runnest before me, shifting every place,
          And darest not stand, nor look me in the face.
          Where art thou now?

[Exit Lysander, following the voice]

[Enter Demetrius]

DEMETRIUS. Lysander, speak again. You run away. You coward, have you fled? Speak! Are you in some bush? Where do you hide your head?

PUCK. *[Sounding like Lysander]* You coward, are you bragging to the stars, telling the bushes that you look for battle, and will not come out? Cowardly boy I'll whip you with a stick. Anyone who draws a sword on you will be disgraced.

DEMETRIUS. Yes, are you there?

PUCK. Follow my voice; we won't fight here.

[Exit]

[Re-enter Lysander]

LYSANDER. He goes in front of me, and still he challenges me. When I get to where he calls, then he is gone. The villain is much faster than I am. I followed quickly, but he did fly even faster. I can't walk without falling on this uneven ground so here will I rest. *[Lies down]* Come, gentle day. If you show me your grey light, I'll find Demetrius and revenge this insult.

[Sleeps]

[Re-enter Puck and Demetrius]

PUCK. Ho, ho, ho! Coward, why do you not come for me?

DEMETRIUS. Face me, if you dare; for well I know that you run from me, hiding in every place, and daring not to stop or look me in the face. Where are you now?

PUCK: Come hither; I am here.

445   DEMETRIUS: Nay, then, thou mock'st me. Thou shalt buy this dear,
If ever I thy face by daylight see;
Now, go thy way. Faintness constraineth me
To measure out my length on this cold bed.
By day's approach look to be visited.

[Lies down and sleeps]

[Enter Helena]

450   HELENA: O weary night, O long and tedious night,
Abate thy hours! Shine comforts from the east,
That I may back to Athens by daylight,
From these that my poor company detest.
And sleep, that sometimes shuts up sorrow's eye,
455   Steal me awhile from mine own company.

[Lies down and sleeps]

PUCK: Yet but three? Come one more;
Two of both kinds makes up four.
Here she comes, curst and sad.
Cupid is a knavish lad,
460   Thus to make poor females mad.

[Enter Hermia]

HERMIA: Never so weary, never so in woe,
Bedabbled with the dew, and torn with briers,
I can no further crawl, no further go;
My legs can keep no pace with my desires.
465   Here will I rest me till the break of day.
Heavens shield Lysander, if they mean a fray!

[Lies down and sleeps]

PUCK: On the ground
Sleep sound;
I'll apply

PUCK. *Come here; I am here.*

DEMETRIUS. *You mock me. You shall pay dearly if ever I face you by daylight. Now go your way. My weary bones force me to stretch out my body on this cold bed. Look to be caught at daybreak.*

[Lies down and sleeps]

[Enter Helena]

HELENA. *O weary night, O long and tedious night, be finished! Shine from the East, so I may go back to Athens by day-light, away from these that my poor mind detests. And sleep, that sometimes closes sad eyes, steal me a while from my own company.*

[Sleeps]

PUCK. *Only three? Here comes another; two of both kinds makes four. Here she comes, fiery and sad. Cupid is a silly boy to make these girls upset.*

[Enter Hermia]

HERMIA. *I never was so weary, never so sorrowful splotched with the dew and torn by thorns. I can not crawl or walk further. My legs cannot keep pace with my desires. Here I will rest until daybreak. Heavens protect Lysander if it looks like a fight!*

[Lies down and sleeps]

PUCK. *Sleep well on the ground I'll apply to each eye, a gentle remedy. [Squeezing the juice on Lysander's eyes] When*

470   To your eye,
             Gentle lover, remedy.
                       [Squeezing the juice on Lysander's eyes]
             When thou wakest,
             Thou takest
475   True delight
             In the sight
             Of thy former lady's eye;
             And the country proverb known,
             That every man should take his own,
480   In your waking shall be shown:
             Jack shall have Jill;
             Nought shall go ill;
The man shall have his mare again, and all shall be well.

                                                    [Exit]

you wake, you will take true delight in the sight of your former lady. As the country proverb says, every man should have his own. By your actions, you shall show that every Jack shall have his Jill. This man shall have his woman again, and all shall be well.

[Exit]

ACT IV

SCENE I
The wood. Lysander, Demetrius,
Helena, and Hermia, lying asleep

[Enter Titania and Bottom; Peaseblossom, Cobweb, Moth, Mustardseed, and other Fairies attending; Oberon behind, unseen]

TITANIA: Come, sit thee down upon this flowery bed,
While I thy amiable cheeks do coy,
And stick musk-roses in thy sleek smooth head,
And kiss thy fair large ears, my gentle joy.

5   BOTTOM: Where's Peaseblossom?

PEASEBLOSSOM: Ready.

BOTTOM: Scratch my head, Peaseblossom. Where's Mounsieur Cobweb?

COBWEB: Ready.

10   BOTTOM: Mounsieur Cobweb; good mounsieur, get you your weapons in your hand and kill me a red-hipped humble-bee on the top of a thistle; and, good mounsieur, bring me the honey-bag. Do not fret yourself too much in the action, mounsieur; and, good mounsieur, have a care the honey-bag break not; I would be loth to have you overflown with a honey-bag, signior. Where's Mounsieur Mustardseed?

15

ACT IV

SCENE I
The wood. Lysander, Demetrius,
Helena, and Hermia, lying asleep

[Enter Titania and Bottom; Peaseblossom, Cobweb, Moth, Mustardseed, and other Fairies attending; Oberon behind, unseen]

TITANIA. *Come, sit down on this flowery bed while I stroke your cheeks and stick roses in your sleek, smooth hair, and kiss your fair large ears, my gentle joy.*

BOTTOM. *Where's Peaseblossom?*

PEASEBLOSSOM. *I'm ready.*

BOTTOM. *Scratch my head, Peaseblossom. Where's Cobweb?*

COBWEB. *I'm ready.*

BOTTOM. *Cobweb; good sir, get your weapons in your hand and kill me a bumblebee on the top of that thistle; and, good sir, bring me its honey-bag. Do not fret about it, sir. And, good sir, be careful that the honey-bag does not break; I would not be happy to have you covered by a honey-bag, sir. Where's Mustardseed?*

MUSTARDSEED: Ready.

BOTTOM: Give me your neaf, Mounsieur Mustardseed. Pray you, leave your courtesy, good mounsieur.

20 MUSTARDSEED: What's your will?

BOTTOM: Nothing, good mounsieur, but to help Cavalery Cobweb to scratch. I must to the barber's, mounsieur; for methinks I am marvellous hairy about the face; and I am such a tender ass, if my hair do but tickle me I must scratch.

25 TITANIA: What, wilt thou hear some music, my sweet love?

BOTTOM: I have a reasonable good ear in music. Let's have the tongs and the bones.

TITANIA: Or say, sweet love, what thou desirest to eat.

BOTTOM: Truly, a peck of provender; I could munch your good dry
30 oats. Methinks I have a great desire to a bottle of hay. Good hay, sweet hay, hath no fellow.

TITANIA: I have a venturous fairy that shall seek
The squirrel's hoard, and fetch thee new nuts.

BOTTOM: I had rather have a handful or two of dried peas. But, I
35 pray you, let none of your people stir me; I have an exposition of sleep come upon me.

TITANIA: Sleep thou, and I will wind thee in my arms.
Fairies, be gone, and be all ways away.
[Exeunt Fairies]
So doth the woodbine the sweet honeysuckle
40 Gently entwist; the female ivy so
Enrings the barky fingers of the elm.
O, how I love thee! how I dote on thee! [They sleep]

MUSTARDSEED. *I'm ready.*

BOTTOM. *Give me your hand, Mustardseed. Don't stand on tradition, sir.*

MUSTARDSEED. *What's your pleasure?*

BOTTOM. *Nothing, except to have you help Cobweb scratch me. I must go to the barber's. I think I am very hairy about the face. I am such an ass that I must scratch when my hair tickles me.*

TITANIA. *Will you hear some music, my sweet love?*

BOTTOM. *I have a reasonably good ear for music. Let's have the instruments.*

TITANIA. *Or say, sweet love, what you wish to eat.*

BOTTOM. *Truly, a quantity of dry food. I could munch your good oats. I thinks I have a great desire for some hay. Good hay, sweet hay, has no equal.*

TITANIA. *I have an adventurous fairy that shall search for the squirrel's hoard and fetch you some nuts.*

BOTTOM. *I would rather have a handful or two of dried peas. But, I pray you, let none of your people stir me; sleep is coming upon me.*

TITANIA. *Sleep, and I will wind you in my arms. Fairies, be gone; away.*

[Exit Fairies]
The vines and sweet honeysuckle gently twist; the female ivy circles the bark of the elm. O, how I love you! How I care for you! *[They sleep]*

[Enter Puck]

OBERON: [Advancing] Welcome, good Robin. See'st thou this sweet
                   sight?
45   Her dotage now I do begin to pity;
           For, meeting her of late behind the wood,
           Seeking sweet favors for this hateful fool,
           I did upbraid her and fall out with her.
           For she his hairy temples then had rounded
50   With coronet of fresh and fragrant flowers;
           And that same dew which sometime on the buds
           Was wont to swell, like round and orient pearls
           Stood now within the pretty flowerets' eyes,
           Like tears, that did their own disgrace bewail.
55   When I had at my pleasure taunted her,
           And she in mild terms begg'd my patience,
           I then did ask of her her changeling child;
           Which straight she gave me, and her fairy sent
           To bear him to my bower in fairy land.
60   And now I have the boy, I will undo
           This hateful imperfection of her eyes.
           And, gentle Puck, take this transformed scalp
           From off the head of this Athenian swain,
           That he awaking when the other do
65   May all to Athens back again repair,
           And think no more of this night's accidents
           But as the fierce vexation of a dream.
           But first I will release the fairy queen.
           [Touching her eyes]
           Be as thou wast wont to be;
70   See as thou was wont to see.
           Dian's bud o'er Cupid's flower
           Hath such force and blessed power.
           Now, my Titania; wake you, my sweet queen.

TITANIA: My Oberon! What visions have I seen!
75   Methought I was enamour'd of an ass.

[Enter Puck]

OBERON. [Advancing] Welcome, good Robin. Do you see this sweet sight? Her love now I do begin to pity. Meeting her lately behind the wood, seeking sweet favors for this stupid fool, I yelled at her and fell out with her. For she has covered his hairy temples with rings of fresh and fragrant flowers. The dew which previously filled small flowers like wonderful pearls now is disgraced. I had taunted her at my pleasure and she-in mild terms-begged for my patience. Then I did ask her for her Indian child. Immediately, she gave the child to me and her fairy was sent to bear him to my home in fairyland. Now that I have the boy, I will undo this hateful imperfection of her eyes. Gentle Puck, take this transformed skull from off the head of this Athenian man so that when he awakens, they may all go back to Athens and think only of this night's accidents as a bad dream. But first I will release the Fairy Queen.

[Touching her eyes]

Be as you were; see as you used to see. This flower will return all to their former ways. Now, my Titania; wake, my sweet queen.

TITANIA. My Oberon! What visions have I seen! I thought I was in love with an ass.

OBERON: There lies your love.

TITANIA: How came these things to pass?
           O, how mine eyes do loathe his visage now!

OBERON: Silence awhile. Robin, take off this head.
80   Titania, music call; and strike more dead
           Than common sleep of all these five the sense.

TITANIA: Music, ho, music, such as charmeth sleep!

PUCK: Now when thou wakest with thine own fool's eyes peep.

OBERON: Sound, music. Come, my Queen, take hands with me,
           [Music]
85   And rock the ground whereon these sleepers be.
           Now thou and I are new in amity,
           And will tomorrow midnight solemnly
           Dance in Duke Theseus' house triumphantly,
           And bless it to all fair prosperity.
90   There shall the pairs of faithful lovers be
           Wedded, with Theseus, an in jollity.

PUCK: Fairy king, attend and mark;
           I do hear the morning lark.

OBERON: Then, my Queen, in silence sad,
95   Trip we after night's shade.
           We the globe can compass soon,
           Swifter than the wandering moon.

TITANIA: Come, my lord; and in our flight,
           Tell me how it came this night
100   That I sleeping here was found
           With these mortals on the ground.
                                   [Exeunt]

OBERON. *There lies your love.*

TITANIA. *How came these things to be? O, how my eyes do hate his face now!*

OBERON. *Silence now. Robin, take off this head. Titania, call music and wake these five from their sleep.*

TITANIA. *Music. Yes, music, a kind that charms sleep!*

PUCK. *Now, when you wake you will see with your own foolish eyes.*

OBERON. *Sound, music. Come, my Queen, hold hands with me, [Music] and rock the ground where these sleepers lie. Now that you and I are new friends again we will dance tomorrow at midnight in Duke Theseus' house and bless with all fair prosperity. There shall the pairs of faithful lovers be wed with great fun.*

PUCK. *Fairy King, attend and listen, I do hear the morning lark.*

OBERON. *Then, my Queen, in somber silence let us follow the night. We can circle the earth more swiftly than the moon.*

TITANIA. *Come, my lord; and during our flight, tell me how it came about that I was found sleeping here with these mortals.*

[Exit]

117

[To the winding of horns, enter Theseus, Hippolyta, Egeus, and train]

THESEUS: Go, one of you, find out the forester;
      For now our observation is perform'd,
      And since we have the vaward of the day,
105   My love shall hear the music of my hounds.
      Uncouple in the western valley; let them go.
      Dispatch, I say, and find the forester.
                      [Exit an Attendant]
      We will, fair queen, up to the mountain's top,
      And mark the musical confusion
110   Of hounds and echo in conjunction.

HIPPOLYTA: I was with Hercules and Cadmus once,
      When in a wood of Crete they bay'd the bear
      With hounds of Sparta; never did I hear
      Such gallant chiding, for, besides the groves,
115   The skies, the fountains, every region near
      Seem'd all one mutual cry. I never heard
      So musical a discord, such sweet thunder.

THESEUS: My hounds are bred out of the Spartan kind,
      So flew'd, so sanded; and their heads are hung
120   With ears that sweep away the morning dew;
      Crook-knee'd and dew-lapp'd like Thessalian bulls;
      Slow in pursuit, but match'd in mouth like bells,
      Each under each. A cry more tuneable
      Was never holla'd to, nor cheer'd with horn,
125   In Crete, in Sparta, nor in Thessaly.
      Judge when you hear. But, soft, what nymphs are these?

EGEUS: My lord, this is my daughter here asleep,
      And this Lysander, this Demetrius is,
      This Helena, old Nedar's Helena.
130   I wonder of their being here together.

THESEUS: No doubt they rose up early to observe
      The rite of May; and, hearing our intent,

[To the blowing of horns, enter Theseus, Hippolyta, Egeus, and train]

THESEUS. Go, one of you, find the forester; for now we have per-
formed our observance and since we have the beginnings of
the day, my love shall hear the music of my dogs. Let them
go; unleash them. Quickly, I say, and find the forester.
                                        [Exit an Attendant]
We will, fair Queen, go up to the mountain's top, and note
the musical confusion my hounds and their echoes make
together.

HIPPOLYTA. I was with Hercules and Cadmus once when in a wood
of Crete they surrounded a bear with hounds from Sparta.
I never heard such gallant sounds. Besides the woods, the
skies, the fountains, every region nearby seemed all one
mutual cry. I never heard so musical a discord, such sweet
thunder.

THESEUS. My hounds are bred from that same breed with their big
jaws, sandy color and heads hung with ears that sweep
away the morning dew. They have crooked knees and their
chins look like bulls' do. They may be slow in pursuit, but
they sound like bells, each similar to each. A nicer sound
was never noted, nor cheered with hunting horns in Crete,
in Sparta, or in Thessaly. Judge them for yourself when
you hear. But, wait; what beauties are these?

EGEUS. My lord, this is my daughter here asleep. This is Lysander;
this Demetrius; this is Helena, old Nedar's Helena. I wonder why they came here together.

THESEUS. No doubt they rose up early to observe the rites of May;
and, hearing our intent to do the same, came here to grace

Came here in grace of our solemnity.
But speak, Egeus; is not this the day

135   That Hermia should give answer of her choice?

EGEUS: It is, my lord.

THESEUS: Go, bid the huntsmen wake them with their horns.
       [Horns and shouting within. The sleepers awake and kneel
       to Theseus]
       Good-morrow, friends. Saint Valentine is past;
       Begin these wood-birds but to couple now?

140   LYSANDER: Pardon, my lord.

THESEUS: I pray you all, stand up.
       I know you two are rival enemies;
       How comes this gentle concord in the world
       That hatred is so far from jealousy

145   To sleep by hate, and fear no enmity?

LYSANDER: My lord, I shall reply amazedly,
       Half sleep, half waking; but as yet, I swear,
       I cannot truly say how I came here,
       But, as I think,—for truly would I speak,

150   And now I do bethink me, so it is,—
       I came with Hermia hither. Our intent
       Was to be gone from Athens, where we might,
       Without the peril of the Athenian law.

EGEUS: Enough, enough, my Lord; you have enough;

155   I beg the law, the law upon his head.
       They would have stolen away, they would, Demetrius,
       Thereby to have defeated you and me:
       You of your wife, and me of my consent,
       Of my consent that she should be your wife.

160   DEMETRIUS: My lord, fair Helen told me of their stealth,
       Of this their purpose hither to this wood;

our solemn rite. But speak, Egeus; is not this the day that Hermia should give the answer to her choice?

EGEUS. *It is, my lord.*

THESEUS. *Go, bid the huntsmen wake them with their horns. [Horns and shout within. The sleepers awake and kneel to Theseus] Good-morning, friends. Saint Valentine's Day is past; do these birds begin to choose mates now?*

LYSANDER. *Pardon, my lord.*

THESEUS. *I pray you all, stand up. I know you two are rivals. How does this gentle agreement work that hatred is so far removed from jealousy that you do not fear to sleep near your enemy?*

LYSANDER. *My lord, I shall reply in amazement. I am half asleep, half-awake; but as yet, I swear, I cannot truly say how I came here. I certainly believe that I came here with Hermia. Our intent was to leave Athens where we might be outside of the dangers of Athenian law.*

EGEUS. *Enough, enough, my lord; you have heard enough. I beg the law, the law enforced upon his head. They would have stolen away. They would, Demetrius, thereby have defeated you and me-you of your wife, and me of my consent; my consent that she should be your wife.*

DEMETRIUS. *My lord, fair Helen told me of their flight to this wood, and, in fury, I followed them; fair Helena following me.*

And I in fury hither followed them,
Fair Helena in fancy following me.
But, my good lord, I wot not by what power,—
165   But by some power it is,—my love to Hermia,
Melted as the snow, seems to me now
As the remembrance of an idle gaud
Which in my childhood I did dote upon;
And all the faith, the virtue of my heart,
170   The object and the pleasure of mine eye,
Is only Helena. To her, my lord,
Was I betroth'd ere I saw Hermia.
But, like a sickness, did I loathe this food;
But, as in health, come to my natural taste,
175   Now I do wish it, love it, long for it,
And will for evermore be true to it.

THESEUS: Fair lovers, you are fortunately met;
Of this discourse we more will hear anon.
Egeus, I will overbear your will;
180   For in the temple, by and by, with us
These couples shall eternally be knit.
And, for the morning now is something worn,
Our purposed hunting shall be set aside.
Away with us to Athens, three and three;
185   We'll hold a feast in great solemnity.
Come, Hippolyta.
       [Exeunt Theseus, Hippolyta, Egeus, and train]

DEMETRIUS: These things seem small and undistinguishable,
Like far-off mountains turned into clouds.

HERMIA: Methinks I see these things with parted eye,
190   When every thing seems double.

HELENA: So methinks;
And I have found Demetrius like a jewel,
Mine own, and not mine own.

But, my good lord, I do not know by what power—but by some power it is—my love for Hermia melted as the snow. It seems to me now as the remembrance of a cheap trinket which in my childhood I loved fondly. The apple of my eye is only Helena. To her, my lord, I was engaged before I saw Hermia. But, like in a sickness, I hated this food. But, I have come to my senses and now I do wish it, love it, long for it, and will forevermore be true to it.

THESEUS. Fair lovers, this is very good news and of this story we will hear more soon. Egeus, I will overrule your will. Soon, with us in the temple, these couples shall eternally be knit. And, since this morning is now somewhat past, our proposed hunt will be called off. Away with us to Athens, all six of us; we'll hold a feast in great solemnity. Come, Hippolyta.

[Exit Theseus, Hippolyta, Egeus, and train]

DEMETRIUS. These things seem small and indistinguishable, like far-off mountains turned into clouds.

HERMIA. I think I see these things with blurry eyes, when everything seems double.

HELENA. So I think I have found Demetrius like a jewel, my own jewel, and yet not my own.

DEMETRIUS: Are you sure
195   That we are awake? It seems to me
           That yet we sleep, we dream. Do not you think
           The Duke was here, and bid us follow him?

HERMIA: Yea, and my father.

HELENA: And Hippolyta.

200 LYSANDER: And he did bid us follow to the temple.

DEMETRIUS: Why, then, we are awake; let's follow him;
           And by the way let us recount our dreams.

                                        [Exeunt]

BOTTOM: [Awaking] When my cue comes, call me, and I will
           answer. My next is 'Most fair Pyramus.' Heigh-ho! Peter
205   Quince! Flute, the bellows-mender! Snout, the tinker!
           Starveling! God's my life, stolen hence, and left me asleep!
           I have had a most rare vision. I have had a dream, past the
           wit of man to say what dream it was. Man is but an ass if he
           go about to expound this dream. Methought I was—there
210   is no man can tell what. Methought I was, and methought
           I had, but man is but a patched fool, if he will offer to say
           what methought I had. The eye of man hath not heard, the
           ear of man hath not seen, man's hand is not able to taste,
           his tongue to conceive, nor his heart to report, what my
215   dream was. I will get Peter Quince to write a ballad of this
           dream. It shall be call'd 'Bottom's Dream,' because it hath no
           bottom; and I will sing it in the latter end of a play, before
           the Duke. Peradventure, to make it the more gracious, I
           shall sing it at her death.

                                        [Exit]

DEMETRIUS. *Are you sure that we are awake? It seems to me that we are still asleep, and we dream. Do you not think the Duke was here, and bid us follow him?*

HERMIA. *Yes, and my father.*

HELENA. *And Hippolyta.*

LYSANDER. *And he did bid us follow to the temple.*

DEMETRIUS. *Why, then, we are awake; let's follow him; along the way, let us recount our dreams.*

[Exit]

BOTTOM. *[Awaking] When my cue comes, call me, and I will answer. My next one is 'Most fair Pyramus.' Well! Peter Quince! Flute, the bellows-mender! Snout, the tinker! Starveling! God, they have stolen away and left me asleep! I have had a most rare vision. I have had a dream beyond the ability of man to say what kind of dream it was. Man is but an ass if he goes about explaining this dream. I thought I was—there is no man who can tell what I was. I thought I was, and I thought I had—but man is a fool if he would offer to say what I thought I had. The eye of man has not heard, the ear of man has not seen, man's hand is not able to taste, his tongue to conceive, nor his heart to report what my dream was. I will get Peter Quince to write a ballad about this dream. It shall be called 'Bottom's Dream,' because it has no bottom; and I will sing it in the latter end of a play before the Duke. Perhaps, to make it more gracious, I shall sing it at her death.*

[Exit]

SCENE II
Athens.
Quince's house

[Enter Quince, Flute, Snout, and Starveling]

QUINCE: Have you sent to Bottom's house? Is he come home yet?

STARVELING: He cannot be heard of. Out of doubt he is transported.

FLUTE: If he come not, then the play is marred; it goes not forward, doth it?

5 QUINCE: It is not possible. You have not a man in all Athens able to discharge Pyramus but he.

FLUTE: No; he hath simply the best wit of any handicraft man in Athens.

QUINCE: Yea, and the best person too; and he is a very paramour for
10 a sweet voice.

FLUTE: You must say 'paragon.' A paramour is- God bless us!—A thing of naught.

[Enter Snug]

SNUG: Masters, the Duke is coming from the temple; and there is two or three lords and ladies more married. If our sport had
15 gone forward, we had all been made men.

FLUTE: O sweet bully Bottom! Thus hath he lost sixpence a day during his life; he could not have scaped sixpence a day.

SCENE II
Athens.
Quince's house

[Enter Quince, Flute, Snout, and Starveling]

QUINCE. Have you checked at Bottom's house? Has he come home yet?

STARVELING. He has not been seen. No doubt he was carried off by spirits.

FLUTE. If he doesn't come, then the play is ruined; it cannot go forward, can it?

QUINCE. It is not possible. There is not a man in all Athens able to act the role of Pyramus except Bottom.

FLUTE. No; he has simply the best ability of any working man in Athens.

QUINCE. Yes, and the best person, too, since he is the very best "lover" with his sweet voice.

FLUTE. You must say 'paragon.' A lover is—God bless us!—A thing of nothingness.

[Enter Snug]

SNUG. Masters, the Duke is coming from the temple with two or three lords and ladies now married. If our play had gone forward, we would all have been made a little wealthier.

FLUTE. O sweet, good Bottom! He lost his good pay for this day. He could not have made this much in another fashion. If the

20 An the Duke had not given him sixpence a day for playing
Pyramus, I'll be hanged. He would have deserved it: sixpence a day in Pyramus, or nothing.

[Enter Bottom]

BOTTOM: Where are these lads? Where are these hearts?

QUINCE: Bottom! O most courageous day! O most happy hour!

BOTTOM: Masters, I am to discourse wonders; but ask me not what;
for if I tell you, I am not true Athenian. I will tell you every-
25 thing, right as it fell out.

QUINCE: Let us hear, sweet Bottom.

BOTTOM: Not a word of me. All that I will tell you is, that the Duke
hath dined. Get your apparel together; good strings to your
beards, new ribbons to your pumps; meet presently at the
30 palace; every man look o'er his part; for the short and the
long is, our play is preferred. In any case, let Thisbe have
clean linen; and let not him that plays the lion pare his
nails, for they shall hang out for the lion's claws. And, most
dear actors, eat no onions nor garlic, for we are to utter
35 sweet breath; and I do not doubt but to hear them say it is a
sweet comedy. No more words. Away, go, away!

[Exeunt]

Duke would not have given him a big amount for playing Pyramus, I'll be hanged. He would have deserved it, a small fortune for playing Pyramus for a day.

[Enter Bottom]

BOTTOM. Where are these lads? Where are these boys?

QUINCE. Bottom! O most wonderful day! O most happy hour!

BOTTOM. Masters, I can tell you of wonders; but ask me not what; for if I tell you, I am no true Athenian. I will tell you everything, right as it happened.

QUINCE. Let us hear, sweet Bottom.

BOTTOM. Not a word from me. All that I can tell you is that the Duke has eaten already. Get your clothes together; string up your beards, put new ribbons in your shoes; gather presently at the palace. Every man look over his part; for the long and short of it is, our play is asked for. In any case, let Thisbe have clean clothes; and let him that plays the lion not cut his nails for they must hang out as if to be lion's claws. And, above all dear actors, do not eat onions or garlic, for we are to utter only sweet breath; since I do not doubt that they will say it is a sweet comedy. No more words. Away, go, away!

[Exit]

ACT V

SCENE I
Athens. The palace of Theseus

[Enter Theseus, Hippolyta, Philostrate, Lords, and Attendants]

HIPPOLYTA: 'Tis strange, my Theseus, that these lovers speak of.

THESEUS: More strange than true. I never may believe
These antique fables, nor these fairy toys.
Lovers and madmen have such seething brains,
Such shaping fantasies, that apprehend
More than cool reason ever comprehends.
The lunatic, the lover, and the poet,
Are of imagination all compact.
One sees more devils than vast hell can hold;
That is the madman. The lover, all as frantic,
Sees Helen's beauty in a brow of Egypt.
The poet's eye, in a fine frenzy rolling,
Doth glance from heaven to earth, from earth to heaven;
And as imagination bodies forth
The forms of things unknown, the poet's pen
Turns them to shapes, and gives to airy nothing
A local habitation and a name.
Such tricks hath strong imagination
That, if it would but apprehend some joy,
It comprehends some bringer of that joy;
Or in the night, imagining some fear,
How easy is a bush supposed a bear?

ACT V

SCENE I
Athens. The palace of Theseus

[Enter Theseus, Hippolyta, Philostrate, Lords, and Attendants]

HIPPOLYTA. It is strange, my Theseus, what these lovers speak of.

THESEUS. More strange than true. I will never believe these antique
fables, nor these fairy tales. Lovers and madmen have
such seething brains, such strange fantasies that captures
more than cool reason ever understands. The lunatic, the
lover, and the poet are all composed of imagination. One
sees more devils than vast hell can hold; that is the madman. The lover, equally as frantic, sees Helen's beauty in a
gypsy's face. The poet's eye, in a fine rolling frenzy, first
glances from heaven to earth, then from earth to heaven;
and as imagination spews forth in the forms of things
unknown, the poet's pen turns them into shapes, and gives
to such airy nothingness a name, a place. Strong imagination has such tricks that, if it would only grasp some joy,
it would understand the creator of that joy. In the night,
imagining some fear, how easy is it then to think that a
bush is a bear?

HIPPOLYTA: But all the story of the night told over,
    And all their minds transfigured so together,
25   More witnesseth than fancy's images,
    And grows to something of great constancy,
    But howsoever strange and admirable.

[Enter Lysander, Demetrius, Hermia, and Helena]

THESEUS: Here come the lovers, full of joy and mirth.
    Joy, gentle friends, joy and fresh days of love
30   Accompany your hearts!

LYSANDER: More than to us
    Wait in your royal walks, your board, your bed!

THESEUS: Come now; what masques, what dances shall we have,
    To wear away this long age of three hours
35   Between our after-supper and bed-time?
    Where is our usual manager of mirth?
    What revels are in hand? Is there no play
    To ease the anguish of a torturing hour?
    Call Philostrate.

40 PHILOSTRATE: Here, mighty Theseus.

THESEUS: Say, what abridgment have you for this evening?
    What masque? what music? How shall we beguile
    The lazy time, if not with some delight?

PHILOSTRATE: There is a brief how many sports are ripe;
45   Make choice of which your Highness will see first.
    [Giving a paper]

THESEUS: 'The battle with the Centaurs, to be sung
    By an Athenian eunuch to the harp.'
    We'll none of that: that have I told my love,
    In glory of my kinsman Hercules.
50   'The riot of the tipsy Bacchanals,

HIPPOLYTA. But with all the story of the night told over and over, and all their minds twisted so together, it is more apparent that fantasies can grow to something of great certainty, however strange and admirable they may seem to be.

[Enter Lysander, Demetrius, Hermia, and Helena]

THESEUS. Here come the lovers, full of joy and mirth. [To the couples] Joy, gentle friends, joy and fresh days of love accompany your hearts!

LYSANDER. The same and more to you, lord.

THESEUS. Come now; what plays, what dances shall we have to wear away this long age of three hours between our evening and bedtime? Where is our usual manager of mirth? What revels are in hand? Is there no play to ease the anguish of a torturing hour? Call Philostrate.

PHILOSTRATE. Here, mighty Theseus.

THESEUS. Say, what treat have you for this evening? What play? What music? How shall we trick this lazy time, if not with some delight?

PHILOSTRATE. There is a paper with possible choices. Make a choice of what your Highness will see first. [Giving a paper]

THESEUS. [Reading from the list] 'The battle with the Centaurs, to be sung by an Athenian eunuch with a harp.' We'll have none of that. I have told of my love of the glory of my kinsman, Hercules. 'The riot of the tipsy Bacchanals, tearing the Thracian singer in their rage.' That is an old piece, and

Tearing the Thracian singer in their rage.'
That is an old device, and it was play'd
When I from Thebes came last a conqueror.
'The thrice three Muses mourning for the death
55   Of Learning, late deceas'd in beggary.'
That is some satire, keen and critical,
Not sorting with a nuptial ceremony.
'A tedious brief scene of young Pyramus
And his love Thisbe; very tragical mirth.'
60   Merry and tragical! tedious and brief!
That is hot ice and wondrous strange snow.
How shall we find the concord of this discord?

PHILOSTRATE: A play there is, my lord, some ten words long,
Which is as brief as I have known a play;
65   But by ten words, my lord, it is too long,
Which makes it tedious; for in all the play
There is not one word apt, one player fitted.
And tragical, my noble lord, it is;
For Pyramus therein doth kill himself.
70   Which when I saw rehearsed, I must confess,
Made mine eyes water; but more merry tears
The passion of loud laughter never shed.

THESEUS: What are they that do play it?

PHILOSTRATE: Hard-handed men that work in Athens here,
75   Which never labour'd in their minds till now;
And now have toil'd their unbreathed memories
With this same play against your nuptial.

THESEUS: And we will hear it.

PHILOSTRATE: No, my noble lord,
80   It is not for you. I have heard it over,
And it is nothing, nothing in the world;
Unless you can find sport in their intents,
Extremely stretch'd and conn'd with cruel pain,
To do you service.

*it was played when I came last from Thebes as a conqueror.
'The nine Muses mourning for the death of Learning,
lately dead from lack of use.' That is some satire, keen and
critical, not fitting for a wedding. 'A tedious brief scene of
young Pyramus and his love Thisbe, very tragic mirth.'
Merry and tragic! Tedious and brief! That is hot ice and
wondrously strange snow. How shall we find the concord
of this discord?*

PHILOSTRATE. *A play there is, my lord, some ten words long, which
is as brief as I have ever known a play; but, my lord, it is
too long, by ten words, which makes it tedious. In all the
play there is not one good word, one player who is fit. And
tragic, my noble lord, it is; for Pyramus kills himself. When
I saw it rehearsed, I must confess, it made my eyes water;
but only tears of great laughter.*

THESEUS. *Who are they that play it?*

PHILOSTRATE. *Hard-handed men who work in Athens here, who
never have used their minds until now. How they have
worked their unused memories with this same play in
preparation for your nuptials.*

THESEUS. *Then we will hear it.*

PHILOSTRATE. *No, my noble lord, it is not for you. I have heard it
over, and it is nothing, nothing in the world, unless you can
find humor in their intention. It is extremely stretched and
strained with cruel pain to do you any good.*

85   THESEUS: I will hear that play;
          For never anything can be amiss
          When simpleness and duty tender it.
          Go, bring them in; and take your places, ladies.
                                 [Exit Philostrate]

    HIPPOLYTA: I love not to see wretchedness o'er-charged,
90   And duty in his service perishing.

    THESEUS: Why, gentle sweet, you shall see no such thing.

    HIPPOLYTA: He says they can do nothing in this kind.

    THESEUS: The kinder we, to give them thanks for nothing.
          Our sport shall be to take what they mistake;
95   And what poor duty cannot do, noble respect
          Takes it in might, not merit.
          Where I have come, great clerks have purposed
          To greet me with premeditated welcomes;
          Where I have seen them shiver and look pale,
100   Make periods in the midst of sentences,
          Throttle their practised accent in their fears,
          And, in conclusion, dumbly have broke off,
          Not paying me a welcome. Trust me, sweet,
          Out of this silence yet I picked a welcome;
          And in the modesty of fearful duty
105   I read as much as from the rattling tongue
          Of saucy and audacious eloquence.
          Love, therefore, and tongue-tied simplicity
          In least speak most to my capacity.

[Re-enter Philostrate]

    PHILOSTRATE: So please your Grace, the Prologue is address'd.

110   THESEUS: Let him approach. [Flourish of trumpets]

THESEUS. *I will hear that play; for never anything can be wrong when simpleness and duty merit it. Go, bring them in; and take your places, ladies.*

[Exit Philostrate]

HIPPOLYTA. *I do not love to see wretchedness overdone and perished in performance of duty.*

THESEUS. *Why, gentle sweet, you shall see no such thing.*

HIPPOLYTA. *He says they can do nothing in this kind.*

THESEUS. *We are kinder still to give them thanks for nothing. Our fun shall be to understand what they mistake; and what their poor actions cannot do, we shall consider their attempt, not their merit. Where I have come from, great clerks have proposed to greet me with premeditated welcomes; I have seen them shiver and look pale and put periods in the middle of sentences, throttling their practiced accents because of their fears. In conclusion, they have dumbly broken off, not paying me a proper welcome. Trust me, sweet, out of this silence yet I picked a welcome. In the modesty of fearful duty I read as much from that as from the rattling tongue of elaborate speeches. Therefore, this tongue-tied simplicity speaks most eloquently in my opinion.*

[Re-enter Philostrate]

PHILOSTRATE. *So please your Grace, the Prologue begins.*

THESEUS. *Let him approach. [Flourish of trumpets]*

[Enter Quince as the Prologue]

PROLOGUE: If we offend, it is with our good will.
That you should think, we come not to offend,
But with good will. To show our simple skill,
That is the true beginning of our end.
115 Consider then, we come but in despite.
We do not come, as minding to content you,
Our true intent is. All for your delight
We are not here. That you should here repent you,
The actors are at band; and, by their show,
120 You shall know all, that you are like to know.

THESEUS: This fellow doth not stand upon points.

LYSANDER: He hath rid his prologue like a rough colt; he knows not
the stop. A good moral, my lord: it is not enough to speak,
but to speak true.

125 HIPPOLYTA: Indeed he hath play'd on this prologue like a child on a
recorder,—a sound, but not in government.

THESEUS: His speech was like a tangled chain; nothing im paired,
but all disordered. Who is next?

[Enter, with a trumpet before them, as in dumb show, Pyramus and
Thisbe, Wall, Moonshine, and Lion]

PROLOGUE: Gentles, perchance you wonder at this show;
130 But wonder on, till truth make all things plain.
This man is Pyramus, if you would know;
This beauteous lady Thisbe is certain.
This man, with lime and rough-cast, doth present
Wall, that vile Wall which did these lovers sunder;
135 And through Wall's chink, poor souls, they are content
To whisper. At the which let no man wonder.

138

[Enter Quince as the Prologue. Speaking spiritedly, but not with correct sentence structure or grammar]

Prologue. If we offend, it is with our good intentions. You should think we come not to offend, except with good intention. To show our simple skill, that is the true beginning of our end. Consider, then, we come only in defiance. We do not come to make you content, which is our true intent. All for your delight we are not here. That you should here "repent" you, the actors are at hand; and, by their show, you shall know all, that you are likely to know.

THESEUS. This fellow does not bother with punctuation.

LYSANDER. He rode this prologue like a rough colt; he knows not where the stop. A good moral, my lord; it is not enough to speak, but to speak accurately.

HIPPOLYTA. Indeed he has played on this prologue like a child on an instrument with sound, but not in control.

THESEUS. His speech was like a tangled chain; nothing broken, but all disorderly. Who is next?

[Enter, with a trumpet before them, as in dumb show, Pyramus and Thisbe, Wall, Moonshine, and Lion]

PROLOGUE. Worthy lords, perchance you wonder at this show; but wonder on, till truth makes all things plain. This man is Pyramus, if you want to know; this is beautiful lady Thisbe. This man, with lime and plaster, does "present" (represent) Wall, that vile Wall which kept these lovers apart; and through Wall's hole, poor souls, they are content to whisper. Let no man wonder at this. This man, with lantern,

139

This man, with lanthorn, dog, and bush of thorn,
Presenteth Moonshine; for, if you will know,
By moonshine did these lovers think no scorn
140   To meet at Ninus' tomb, there, there to woo.
This grisly beast, which Lion hight by name,
The trusty Thisbe, coming first by night,
Did scare away, or rather did affright;
And as she fled, her mantle she did fall;
145   Which Lion vile with bloody mouth did stain.
Anon comes Pyramus, sweet youth and tall,
And finds his trusty Thisbe's mantle slain;
Whereat with blade, with bloody blameful blade,
He bravely broach'd his boiling bloody breast;
150   And Thisbe, tarrying in mulberry shade,
His dagger drew, and died. For all the rest,
Let Lion, Moonshine, Wall, and lovers twain,
At large discourse while here they do remain.

[Exeunt Prologue, Pyramus, Thisbe, Lion, and Moonshine]

THESEUS: I wonder if the lion be to speak.

155   DEMETRIUS: No wonder, my lord: one lion may, when many asses
    do.

WALL: In this same interlude it doth befall
    That I, one Snout by name, present a wall;
    And such a wall as I would have you think
    That had in it a crannied hole or chink,
160   Through which the lovers, Pyramus and Thisbe,
    Did whisper often very secretly.
    This loam, this rough-cast, and this stone, doth show
    That I am that same wall; the truth is so;
    And this the cranny is, right and sinister,
165   Through which the fearful lovers are to whisper.

THESEUS: Would you desire lime and hair to speak better?

*dog, and thornbush "presents" (represents) Moonshine; for,
you should know, by moonshine did these lovers think it
fine to meet at Ninus' tomb, and there, there to court.
This grisly beast, which is called Lion by name, the trusty
Thisbe, coming first by night, did scare away, or rather
frightened. As she fled, her cloak she dropped and the Lion
stained it with its bloody mouth. Soon comes Pyramus,
sweet youth and tall, and finds his trusty Thisbe's cloak
slain. Then with blade, with bloody blameful blade, he
bravely approached this boiling bloody breast; and Thisbe,
tarrying in the mulberry tree's shade, drew his dagger, and
died. For all the rest, let Lion, Moonshine, Wall, and two
lovers speak.*

[Exit Prologue, Pyramus, Thisbe, Lion, and Moonshine]

THESEUS. *I wonder if the lion will speak.*

DEMETRIUS. *Don't wonder, my lord, one lion certainly may, since so
many asses already do.*

WALL. *In this same interlude it does begin that I, one Snout by
name, "presents" a wall; in such a wall it contains a cran-
nied hole or chink through which the lovers, Pyramus and
Thisbe, did whisper often very secretly. This dirt, this plaster, and this stone show that I am that same wall; the truth
is so; and this is the cranny, right and left, through which
the fearful lovers are to whisper.*

THESEUS. *Could you ask lime and hair to speak better than this?*

141

DEMETRIUS: It is the wittiest partition that ever I heard discourse, my lord.

[Enter Pyramus]

THESEUS: Pyramus draws near the wall; silence.

170 PYRAMUS: O grim-look'd night! O night with hue so black!
O night, which ever art when day is not!
O night, O night, alack, alack, alack,
I fear my Thisbe's promise is forgot!
And thou, O wall, O sweet, O lovely wall,
175 That stand'st between her father's ground and mine;
Thou wall, O wall, O sweet and lovely wall,
Show me thy chink, to blink through with mine eyne.
[Wall holds up his fingers]
Thanks, courteous wall. Jove shield thee well for this!
But what see I? No Thisbe do I see.
180 O wicked wall, through whom I see no bliss,
Curs'd he thy stones for thus deceiving me!

THESEUS: The wall, methinks, being sensible, should curse again.

PYRAMUS: No, in truth, sir, he should not. Deceiving me is Thisbe's cue. She is to enter now, and I am to spy her through the
185 wall. You shall see it will fall pat as I told you; yonder she comes.

[Enter Thisbe]

THISBE: O wall, full often hast thou beard my moans,
For parting my fair Pyramus and me!
My cherry lips have often kiss'd thy stones,
190 Thy stones with lime and hair knit up in thee.

DEMETRIUS. *It is the wittiest partition that ever I have heard speak, my lord.*

[Enter Pyramus]

THESEUS. *[To audience] Pyramus draws near the wall; silence.*

PYRAMUS. *O grim-looking night! O night with colors so black! O night, which is all that day is not! O night, O night! Alas, alas, alas! I fear my Thisbe's promise is forgotten! And you, O wall, O sweet, O lovely wall, that stands between her father's grounds and mine. Wall, O wall, O sweet and lovely wall, show me your hole to blink through with my eyes. [Wall holds up his fingers] Thanks, courteous wall. May the gods protect you well for this! But what do I see? I see no Thisbe. O wicked wall, through whom I see no bliss; cursed be your stones for deceiving me!*

THESEUS. *The wall, I think, being sensible, should curse again.*

PYRAMUS. *[Speaking to Theseus] No, in truth, sir, he should not. "Deceiving me" is Thisbe's cue. She is to enter now, and I am to spy her through the wall. You shall see. It will fall in place as I told you; here she comes.*

[Enter Thisbe]

THISBE. *O wall, full often have you heard my moans, since you separate my fair Pyramus and me! My cherry lips have often kissed your stones, stones with lime and hair.*

PYRAMUS: I see a voice; now will I to the chink,
To spy an I can hear my Thisbe's face.
Thisbe!

THISBE: My love! thou art my love, I think.

195 PYRAMUS: Think what thou wilt, I am thy lover's grace;
And like Limander am I trusty still.

THISBE: And I like Helen, till the Fates me kill.

PYRAMUS: Not Shafalus to Procrus was so true.

THISBE: As Shafalus to Procrus, I to you.

200 PYRAMUS: O, kiss me through the hole of this vile wall.

THISBE: I kiss the wall's hole, not your lips at all.

PYRAMUS: Wilt thou at Ninny's tomb meet me straightway?

THISBE: 'Tide life, 'tide death, I come without delay.
[Exeunt Pyramus and Thisbe]

205 WALL: Thus have I, wall, my part discharged so;
And, being done, thus Wall away doth go.
[Exit Wall]

THESEUS: Now is the mural down between the two neighbors.

DEMETRIUS: No remedy, my lord, when walls are so wilful to hear
without warning.

HIPPOLYTA: This is the silliest stuff that ever I heard.

PYRAMUS. *I see a voice; now will I go to the hole to spy and I can hear my Thisbe's face. Thisbe!*

THISBE. *My love! You are my love, I think.*

PYRAMUS. *Think what you will, I am your lover; and like "Limander" I am still trustworthy.*

THISBE. *And I am like Helen until the Fates kill me.*

PYRAMUS. *No Shafalus to Procrus was ever so true.*

THISBE. *As Shafalus was to Procrus, I am true to you.*

PYRAMUS. *O, kiss me through the hole of this vile wall.*

THISBE. *I kiss the wall's hole, not your lips at all.*

PYRAMUS. *Will you meet me at Ninny's tomb immediately?*

THISBE. *Come life, come death, I come without delay.*
[Exit Pyramus and Thisbe]

WALL. *Thus have I, Wall, finished my part; and, being done, thus Wall goes away.*
[Exit Wall]

THESEUS. *Now is the moon used between the two neighbors.*

DEMETRIUS. *No remedy, my lord, when walls are so eager to hear.*

HIPPOLYTA. *This is the silliest stuff that I ever have heard.*

210 THESEUS: The best in this kind are but shadows; and the worst are
        no worse, if imagination amend them.

HIPPOLYTA: It must be your imagination then, and not theirs.

THESEUS: If we imagine no worse of them than they of themselves,
        they may pass for excellent men. Here come two noble
215   beasts in, a man and a lion.

[Enter Lion and Moonshine]

LION: You, ladies, you, whose gentle hearts do fear
        The smallest monstrous mouse that creeps on floor,
        May now, perchance, both quake and tremble here,
        When lion rough in wildest rage doth roar.
220   Then know that I, as Snug the joiner, am
        A lion fell, nor else no lion's dam;
        For, if I should as lion come in strife
        Into this place, 'twere pity on my life.

THESEUS: A very gentle beast, and of a good conscience.

225 DEMETRIUS: The very best at a beast, my lord, that e'er I saw.

LYSANDER: This lion is a very fox for his valour.

THESEUS: True; and a goose for his discretion.

DEMETRIUS: Not so, my lord; for his valour cannot carry his discre-
        tion, and the fox carries the goose.

230 THESEUS: His discretion, I am sure, cannot carry his valour; for the
        goose carries not the fox. It is well. Leave it to his discre-
        tion, and let us listen to the moon.

146

THESEUS. The best of these actors are mere shadows; and the worst are not really worse if your imagination can fix them.

HIPPOLYTA. It must be your imagination then, and not theirs.

THESEUS. If we think no worse of them than they do of themselves, they might pass for excellent men. Here come two noble beasts—a man and a lion.

[Enter Lion and Moonshine]

LION. You, ladies, you, whose gentle hearts do fear the smallest, monstrous mouse that creeps on the floor, may now, perhaps, both shake and tremble here when a rough lion roars in wildest rage. Please know that I am known as Snug, the joiner. I appear as a fierce male lion; but if I should come here as a lion in anger it would cost me my life.

THESEUS. A very polite beast, and of a good conscience.

DEMETRIUS. The very best at playing a beast, my lord, that ever I have seen.

LYSANDER. This lion is certainly more crafty than courageous.

THESEUS. True; and certainly more silly than crafty.

DEMETRIUS. Not so, my lord; for his courage cannot carry his craftiness and the fox surely carries the goose.

THESEUS. His craftiness, I am sure, cannot carry his courage; for the goose does not carry the fox. It is well. Leave it with his craftiness, and let us listen to the Moon.

MOONSHINE: This lanthorn doth the horned moon present—

DEMETRIUS: He should have worn the horns on his head.

235 THESEUS: He is no crescent, and his horns are invisible within the
circumference.

MOONSHINE: This lanthorn doth the horned moon present;
Myself the Man i' the moon do seem to be.

THESEUS: This is the greatest error of all the rest; the man should be
240 put into the lantern. How is it else the man i' the moon?

DEMETRIUS: He dares not come there for the candle; for, you see, it
is already in snuff.

HIPPOLYTA: I am aweary of this moon. Would he would change!

245 THESEUS: It appears, by his small light of discretion, that he is in the
wane; but yet, in courtesy, in all reason, we must stay the
time.

LYSANDER: Proceed, Moon.

MOON: All that I have to say is to tell you that the lanthorn is the
moon; I, the man i' the moon; this thorn-bush, my thorn-
250 bush; and this dog, my dog.

DEMETRIUS: Why, all these should be in the lantern; for all these are
in the moon. But silence; here comes Thisbe.

[Re-enter Thisbe]

THISBE: This is old Ninny's tomb. Where is my love?

LION: [Roaring] O—   [Thisbe runs off]

MOONSHINE. *This lantern represents the horned moon.*

DEMETRIUS. *He should have worn the horns on his head.*

THESEUS. *But he has no crescent, and his horns are invisible.*

MOONSHINE. *This lantern represents the horned moon. I am the man in the moon.*

THESEUS. *This is the greatest error of all; this man should be put inside the lantern. How else is he the man in the moon?*

DEMETRIUS. *He dares not go there because of the candle; for, you see, it is already hot.*

HIPPOLYTA. *I am weary of this moon. I wish he would change!*

THESEUS. *It appears, by his small light of common sense that he is already growing small; but yet, for courtesy's sake, we must remain a while.*

LYSANDER. *Proceed, Moon.*

MOON. *All that I have to say is to tell you that the lantern is the moon; I, the man in the Moon; this thornbush is my thornbush; and this dog is my dog.*

DEMETRIUS. *Why, all these should be inside the lantern; for all these are in the moon. But silence; here comes Thisbe.*

[Re-enter Thisbe]

THISBE. *This is old Ninny's tomb. Where is my love?*

LION. *[Roaring] O— [Thisbe runs off]*

255   DEMETRIUS: Well roared, Lion.

THESEUS: Well run, Thisbe.

HIPPOLYTA: Well shone, Moon. Truly, the moon shines with a good
        grace.

                   [The Lion tears Thisbe's mantle, and exit]

260   THESEUS: Well moused, Lion.

DEMETRIUS: And then came Pyramus.

LYSANDER: And so the lion vanished.

[Re-enter Pyramus]

PYRAMUS: Sweet Moon, I thank thee for thy sunny beams;
        I thank thee, Moon, for shining now so bright;
265   For, by thy gracious, golden, glittering gleams,
          I trust to take of truest Thisbe sight.
           But stay, O spite!
           But mark, poor knight,
        What dreadful dole is here!
270   Eyes, do you see?
          How can it he?
        O dainty duck! O dear!
          Thy mantle good,
        What! stain'd with blood?
275   Approach, ye Furies fell.
          O Fates! come, come;
          Cut thread and thrum;
        Quail, crush, conclude, and quell.

THESEUS: This passion, and the death of a dear friend, would go
280   near to make a man look sad.

DEMETRIUS. *Well roared, Lion.*

THESEUS. *Well run, Thisbe!*

HIPPOLYTA. *Well shone, Moon. Truly, the moon shines with a good grace.*

[*The Lion tears Thisbe's Mantle, and exit*]

THESEUS. *Well tossed, Lion!*

DEMETRIUS. *And then came Pyramus.*

LYSANDER. *And so the lion vanished.*

[*Re-enter Pyramus*]

PYRAMUS. *Sweet Moon, I thank you for your sunny beams; I thank you, Moon, for shining now so bright. By your gracious, golden, glitterings, I trust I will see Thisbe. But stay, O spite! But mark, poor knight, What a dreadful sight is here! Eyes, do you see? How can it be? O dainty duck! O dear! Your cloak-good, What! Stained with blood? Approach, you fierce Furies. O Fates! come, come; Cut thread and life; Squash, Crush. Conclude. And kill.*

THESEUS. *This sorrow at the death of a dear friend would certainly make a man look sad.*

HIPPOLYTA: Beshrew my heart, but I pity the man.

PYRAMUS: O wherefore, Nature, didst thou lions frame?
   Since lion vile hath here deflower'd my dear;
  Which is—no, no—which was the fairest dame
285   That lived, that loved, that liked, that looked with cheer.
    Come, tears, confound;
    Out, sword, and wound
   The pap of Pyramus;
    Ay, that left pap,
290   Where heart doth hop. [Stabs himself]
   Thus die I, thus, thus, thus.
    Now am I dead,
    Now am I fled;
   My soul is in the sky.
295   Tongue, lose thy light;
    Moon, take thy flight.
         [Exit Moonshine]
   Now die, die, die, die, die. [Dies]

DEMETRIUS: No die, but an ace, for him; for he is but one.

LYSANDER: Less than an ace, man; for he is dead; he is nothing.

300 THESEUS: With the help of a surgeon he might yet recover and yet
    prove an ass.

HIPPOLYTA: How chance Moonshine is gone before Thisbe comes
    back and finds her lover?

THESEUS: She will find him by starlight. Here she comes; and her
    passion ends the play.

[Re-enter Thisbe]

Hippolyta. Woe is my heart, but I would certainly pity that man.

Pyramus. O why, Nature, did you make a lion since a lion's evil killed my dear. She is—no, no—she was the fairest lady who ever lived, who loved, who liked, who looked so cheerful. Come, tears, confound; Out, sword, and wound The chest of Pyramus. Yes, that left chest, Where the heart hops. [Stabs himself] Thus I die, thus, thus, thus. Now I am dead, Now I am fled; My soul is in the sky. Tongue, lose your light; Moon, take our flight.

[Exit Moonshine]
Now die, die, die, die, die.   [Dies]

DEMETRIUS. [Using gambling terms] No die, but an ace, for him; for he is only an ass.

LYSANDER. Less than an ace, man; for he is dead; he is nothing.

THESEUS. With the help of a surgeon he might still recover and yet prove to be an ass.

HIPPOLYTA. Why has Moonshine gone before Thisbe comes back and finds her lover?

THESEUS. She will find him by starlight. Here she comes; and her passion ends the play.

[Re-enter Thisbe]

305 HIPPOLYTA: Methinks she should not use a long one for such a
        Pyramus; I hope she will be brief.

    DEMETRIUS: A mote will turn the balance, which Pyramus, which
        Thisbe, is the better,—he for a man, God warrant us: She
        for a woman, God bless us!

310 LYSANDER: She hath spied him already with those sweet eyes.

    DEMETRIUS: And thus she moans, videlicet:—

    THISBE: Asleep, my love?
                    What, dead, my dove?
                     O Pyramus, arise,
315   Speak, speak. Quite dumb?
                    Dead, dead? A tomb
                     Must cover thy sweet eyes.
                    These lily lips,
                    This cherry nose,
320   These yellow cowslip cheeks,
                    Are gone, are gone;
                    Lovers, make moan;
                     His eyes were green as leeks.
                    O Sisters Three,
325   Come, come to me,
                     With hands as pale as milk;
                    Lay them in gore,
                    Since you have shore
                     With shears his thread of silk.
330   Tongue, not a word.
                    Come, trusty sword;
                     Come, blade, my breast imbrue.
                                            [Stabs herself]
                    And farewell, friends;
                    Thus Thisbe ends;
335   Adieu, adieu, adieu.   [Dies]

HIPPOLYTA. *I think she should not have as long a speech as Pyramus;*
I hope she will be brief.

DEMETRIUS. *A tiny thing will decide whether Pyramus or Thisbe is*
the better actor—he for a man, God help us—or she for a
woman,—God bless us!

LYSANDER. *She has spied him already with those sweet eyes.*

DEMETRIUS. *And thus she moans-*

THISBE.   *Asleep, my love?*
            What, dead, my dove?
        O Pyramus, arise,
            Speak, speak. Quite dumb?
        Dead, dead? A tomb
    Must cover your sweet eyes,
            These lily lips,
            This cherry nose,
    These yellow rose cheeks,
        Are gone, are gone;
        Lovers, make moan;
    His eyes were green as onions.
        O these Fates, Come, come to me,
    With hands as pale as milk;
            Lay them in blood,
        Since you have cut
    With shears his thread of silk.
        Tongue, do not say a word.
        Come, trusty sword;
    Come, blade, color my breast.
                                    [Stabs herself]

            And farewell, friends;
        Thus Thisbe ends;
    Good-bye, good-bye, good-bye.
                                    [Dies]

155

THESEUS: Moonshine and Lion are left to bury the dead.

DEMETRIUS: Ay, and Wall too.

BOTTOM: [Starting up] No, I assure you; the wall is down that
340   parted their fathers. Will it please you to see the epilogue,
              or to hear a Bergomask dance between two of our company?

THESEUS: No epilogue, I pray you; for your play needs no excuse.
              Never excuse; for when the players are all dead there need
              none to be blamed. Marry, if he that writ it had played
              Pyramus, and hanged himself in Thisbe's garter, it would
345   have been a fine tragedy. And so it is, truly; and very nota-
              bly discharged. But come, your Bergomask; let your epi-
              logue alone.
              [A dance]
              The iron tongue of midnight hath told twelve.
350   Lovers, to bed; 'tis almost fairy time.
              I fear we shall out-sleep the coming morn,
              As much as we this night have overwatch'd.
              This palpable-gross play hath well beguiled
              The heavy gait of night. Sweet friends, to bed.
355   A fortnight hold we this solemnity,
              In nightly revels and new jollity.

                                [Exeunt]

[Enter Puck with a broom]

PUCK: Now the hungry lion roars,
              And the wolf behowls the moon;
              Whilst the heavy ploughman snores,
360   All with weary task fordone.
              Now the wasted brands do glow,
                Whilst the screech-owl, screeching loud,
              Puts the wretch that lies in woe
                In remembrance of a shroud.
365   Now it is the time of night

THESEUS. Moonshine and Lion are left to bury the dead.

DEMETRIUS. Yes, and Wall, too.

BOTTOM. [Sitting up] No, I assure you; the wall has fallen that parted their fathers. Will it please you to "see" the Epilogue, or
to "hear" an Italian dance from two of our company?

THESEUS. No epilogue, please, for your play needs no more stretch-
ing. Not more; for when the players are all dead there are
none left to be blamed. Well, if the man who wrote this had
played Pyramus, and hanged himself with Thisbe's stock-
ing, it would've been a fine tragedy. Yes, indeed; and very
memorable, too. But now, your dance; forget the epilogue.
[A dance]
It is after midnight, lover. To bed; it is almost fairy time. I
fear we shall sleep in tomorrow since it is so very late. This
ridiculous play has well transported us through the night.
Sweet friends, to bed. We can continue this fun over the
next few weeks.

[Exit]

[Enter Puck with a broom]

PUCK. Now the hungry lion roars, and the wolf howls at the moon;
all the while, the tired farmer works at his task of snor-
ing. Now the last embers of logs glow while the screech-
owl screams its song of death. Now it is the time of night
when graves open wide and every one lets forth a spirit to
glide down the church paths. We fairies, who are run by
the Spirits, move from the presence of the light following
darkness like a dream, have great fun. Not even a mouse

That the graves, all gaping wide,
Every one lets forth his sprite,
In the church-way paths to glide.
And we fairies, that do run
370   By the triple Hecate's team
From the presence of the sun,
Following darkness like a dream,
Now are frolic. Not a mouse
Shall disturb this hallow'd house.
375   I am sent with broom before,
To sweep the dust behind the door.

[Enter Oberon and Titania, with all their train]

OBERON: Through the house give glimmering light,
By the dead and drowsy fire;
Every elf and fairy sprite
380   Hop as light as bird from brier;
And this ditty, after me,
Sing and dance it trippingly.

TITANIA: First, rehearse your song by rote,
To each word a warbling note;
385   Hand in hand, with fairy grace,
Will we sing, and bless this place.

[Oberon leading, the Fairies sing and dance]

OBERON: Now, until the break of day,
Through this house each fairy stray.
To the best bride-bed will we,
390   Which by us shall blessed be;
And the issue there create
Ever shall be fortunate.
So shall all the couples three
Ever true in loving be;
395   And the blots of Nature's hand
Shall not in their issue stand;

will disturb this hallowed home. I am sent before all with a broom to sweep the dust behind the door.

[Enter Oberon and Titania, with all their train]

OBERON. Enjoy the glimmering light near the dying fire; every elf and fairy spirit will now hop as lightly as a bird; and this little song sing and dance to it.

TITANIA. First, rehearse your song by memorizing each word and warbling note. Hand in hand, we will sing we sing and bless this house with fairy grace.

[Oberon leading, the Fairies sing and dance]

OBERON. Until the break of day every fairy shall fly through this house. We will go to the best bride-bed, which we shall bless and the child that is begun there will ever be fortunate. So shall all these three couples ever be truly in love and the blots of Nature shall not form in their children. No deformity which humans despise shall these children have at birth. [Gathering dewdrops] Bless with this dew. Every fairy should go on his own path and bless several chambers

Never mole, hare-lip, nor scar,
Nor mark prodigious, such as are
Despised in nativity,
400 Shall upon their children be.
With this field-dew consecrate,
Every fairy take his gait,
And each several chamber bless,
Through this palace, with sweet peace;
405 And the owner of it blest
Ever shall in safety rest.
Trip away; make no stay;
Meet me all by break of day.

[Exeunt all but Puck]

PUCK: If we shadows have offended,
410 Think but this, and all is mended,
That you have but slumber'd here
While these visions did appear.
And this weak and idle theme,
No more yielding but a dream,
415 Gentles, do not reprehend.
If you pardon, we will mend.
And, as I am an honest Puck,
If we have unearned luck
Now to scape the serpent's tongue,
420 We will make amends ere long;
Else the Puck a liar call.
So, good night unto you all.
Give me your hands, if we be friends,
And Robin shall restore amends.   [Exit]

THE END

through this palace with sweet peace. The owner of it will ever be blessed with secure rest. Get moving; do not stay. We will meet at daybreak.

[Exit all but Puck]

PUCK. *If we spirits have offended anyone, all is mended if you merely think you have only slept here while these visions appeared, and this play is no more than a dream. Do not be angry with us; if you ask, we will fix it all. And, as I am an honest Puck, if we have not deserved to escape the hissing of the audience, we will make amends before long. Otherwise, call Puck a liar. So, good night to you all. Applaud if we are friends, and Robin shall restore all.*

[Exit]

THE END

Study Guide

Act I, Scene 1 (Athens, the Duke's palace)

1. As Theseus eagerly awaits his marriage day, four days hence, what does he tell Philostrate to do regarding the residents of Athens?

2. In the same speech, what do we learn of the earlier relationship between Theseus and Hippolyta?

3. Of what does Egeus accuse Lysander?

4. What does Egeus request of the Duke?

5. What does Theseus say is Hermia's responsibility?

6. In her responses to the Duke, what kind of person does Hermia show herself to be?

7. Hermia speaks and give the first of many mentions to "eye." What juxtaposition is set up by this?

8. In his response to her question, what does the Duke tell Hermia may happen to her if she continues to refuse to obey?

9. In the last line of his speech to the Duke, why does Lysander call Demetrius inconstant?

10. The Duke, admits having heard this, but has been too consumed with his own affairs, and prepares to leave the room. What ultimatum does he give Hermia?

11. The Duke has told Hermia what the law is and that it will be followed. From his behavior and manner, what do you think the Duke represents?

12. In the exchange that follows between Lysander and Hermia, what do they say impedes "the course of true love"? List 6 impediments.

13. What plan does Lysander propose in order to marry Hermia?

14. What does Helena suggest is love's attraction?

15. What are Helena's comments on love near the end of Scene 1?

16. What plan of action does Helena decide to take?

17. What is the setting for this first scene? What does the setting suggest?

18. Explain what these characters say about love:

    A.   Theseus and Hippolyta

    B.   Hermia and Lysander

    C.   Demetrius

    D.   Helena

19. Some readers complain that it is hard to tell the four lovers apart because they all seem to talk and think alike. What might be a reason for this?

Act I, Scene 2 (Athens, a laborer's home)

1. Although Peter Quince seems to be the designated leader or director in this group of workmen, what draws our attention to Nick Bottom?

2. What do they fear may happen if they are not careful when they portray the lion?

3. What makes the reader believe that this is not a realistic appraisal of the situation?

4. Why is the group rehearsing a play?

5. What characterizes the language of Nick Bottom and the others?

6. Despite his faults, what makes Bottom a likable character?

Act II, Scene 1 (A woods outside of Athens)

1. Puck sets up the scene for the reader. What does he say is the cause of the dispute between Oberon and Titania?

2. What has happened as a result of this dispute?

3. What seems to be the reason behind Puck's pranks?

4. What, according to Titania, is Oberon's problem?

5. What does Titania say has happened as a result of their dispute?

6. Why will Titania not give up the boy?

7. What does Oberon sends Puck to get?

8. What does he plan to do with this potion?

9. What opinion of Helena and Demetrius do you get in their exchange?

10. What further instructions does Oberon give Puck?

11. Why do you suppose Oberon cares about helping Helena?

Act II, Scene 2 (The same woods)

1. What is Hermia's response to Lysander's suggestion that they lie down together?

2. Mistakenly, Puck puts the potion on Lysander's eyes rather than on Demetrius'. What may come of this?

3. Who awakens Lysander and what happens?

4. How does Lysander explain his change of heart?

5. What, in fact, caused the change in Lysander's affections?

6. What is Helena's response to Lysander's declarations of love? Why?

7. What is the setting for this act and what is associated with this setting?

Act III, Scene 1 (The same woods)

1. This scene again brings up the idea of reality and illusion, particularly as it applies to the theater. How do the workmen/players fear that their theatrical illusion may be mistaken for reality?

2. While the players' fears are silly, because no one will confuse their illusion with reality, how does Shakespeare trick us into believing in the reality of Nick Bottom?

3. When Bottom comes on stage again, Quince tells everyone to run off. Why?

4. What is Bottom's reaction to their running off? What does he conclude?

5. Titania, hearing Bottom singing, awakens. What is her reaction?

6. What is Bottom's response to Titania's declaration?

7. How would you characterize Bottom's dialogue with the fairies?

8. What does Titania suggest that she sees as one fault of Bottom?

Act III, Scene 2 (the same woods)

1. Near the beginning of the scene, why does Hermia reprimand Demetrius?

2. What does Puck's response demonstrate?

3. In order to return the situation to normal, the potion is put on Demetrius' eyes. Puck is sent to bring Helena to Demetrius, so that she may be the first thing he sees when he wakes. As they wait, Puck says, "Lord, what fool these mortals be!" What prompts this observation?

4. Demetrius awakens and vows his love for Helena. What is Helena's response?

5. When Hermia appears, why does Helena think that all three of her friends have joined together to make fun of her?

6. Why is Helena's speech especially poignant?

7. When Hermia finally realizes that Lysander no longer loves her, what is her reaction to his love for Helena?

8. Having lost her beloved, how does Hermia now see herself?

9. What does Oberon tell Puck to do to get these problems Puck caused straightened out?

10. What does Hermia's comment reveal about the depth of her love?

11. In your opinion, if Lysander's love were a true love, could a potion change it so drastically? Does Puck make fools of the lovers, or is Shakespeare saying that humans in love behave like fools?

12. The scene raises one question a number of times: what do we see when we look at the one we love? Do we see that person, or do we see only our own vision of the person? What, on the other hand, do we see when, like Lysander, we fall out of love?

Act IV, Scene 1 (The same woods)

1. As this scene opens, what is the picture we get of Bottom?

2. How do their choices in music further contrast the difference between Titania and Bottom?

3. The word "dote" comes up several times; in this scene it is used by Titania. Remember that earlier, Helena talked of doting on Demetrius. What does this word suggest?

4. What does Oberon's reaction to Titania's doting on Bottom seem to be?

5. Once Oberon gets the changeling boy from Titania, what is the Fairy King's plan for Bottom?

6. How does Lysander's comment, reinforce the theme?

7. What is the main idea in of Demetrius' speech to Egeus?

8. Why do the lovers question whether they are asleep or not?

9. What is their conclusion?

10. What is Bottom's reaction when he wakes?

11. What is significant about the fact that this scene ends with the four lovers going off to celebrate Theseus' wedding, and their own?

12. Throughout the play moonlight is mentioned over 20 times. With what concept are we meant to associate the moon and moonlight?

Act IV, Scene 2 (Athens, Quince's house)

1. Why can't Bottom make up his mind about telling or not telling his friends what has happened to him?

Act V, Scene 1 (Athens, Theseus' palace)

1. Hippolyta finds the story related by the lovers strange. What is Theseus' reaction to it?

2. What do the poets, madmen, and lovers have in common, especially as it relates to a theme for the play of reality intertwining with illusion?

3. Although he has been warned that it is a terrible play, why does Theseus insist on seeing it?

4.   Hippolyta is concerned that these players might embarrass themselves, and that laughing at their effort would be unkind. Theseus compares their efforts at play-making to someone who wishes to speak to him, but becomes tongue-tied. What is the point of comparison he is making? As a result, what is our opinion of Theseus?

5.   Briefly, what is the plot of the play-within-a-play, "Pyramus and Thisbe"?

6.   How does this tragedy of Pyramus and Thisbe give a comical reflection to the main plot?

7.   Critics point out that to be really appreciated, this last act must be overacted? Why do you suppose they say this?

8.   Why is it somewhat ironic that Lysander and Demetrius should be laughing at the troubles of Pyramus and Thisbe?

9.   As the three pair of lovers, now all united in marriage, march off the stage, the reunited Oberon and Titania appear. What is the tone and substance of their comments?

10.   According to Puck, what should someone who is offended by "A Midsummer Night's Dream" think of it?

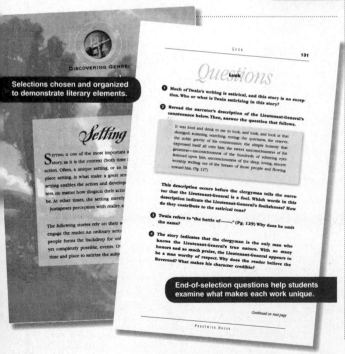

Insightful and Reader-Friendly, Yet Affordable

Prestwick House Literary Touchstone Classic Editions– The Editions By Which All Others May Be Judged

Every *Prestwick House Literary Touchstone Classic* is enhanced with Reading Pointers for Sharper Insight to improve comprehension and provide insights that will help students recognize key themes, symbols, and plot complexities. In addition, each title includes a Glossary of the more difficult words and concepts.

For the Shakespeare titles, along with the Reading Pointers and Glossary, we include margin notes and various strategies to understanding the language of Shakespeare.

New titles are constantly being added; call or visit our website for current listing.

Special Educator's Discount – At Least

50% Off

			Retail Price	Educator's Discount
200053	Adventures of Huckleberry Finn		$4.99	**$2.49**
202118	Antigone		$3.99	**$1.99**
200141	Awakening, The		$5.99	**$2.99**
200179	Christmas Carol, A		$3.99	**$1.99**
200694	Doll's House, A		$3.99	**$1.99**
200054	Frankenstein		$4.99	**$1.99**
200091	Hamlet		$3.99	**$1.99**
200074	Heart of Darkness		$3.99	**$1.99**
200147	Importance of Being Earnest, The		$3.99	**$1.99**
200146	Julius Caesar		$3.99	**$1.99**
200125	Macbeth		$3.99	**$1.99**
200081	Midsummer Night's Dream, A		$3.99	**$1.99**
200079	Narrative of the Life of Frederick Douglass		$3.99	**$1.99**
200564	Oedipus Rex		$3.99	**$1.99**
200095	Othello		$3.99	**$1.99**
200193	Romeo and Juliet		$3.99	**$0.99**
200132	Scarlet Letter, The		$5.99	**$2.99**
200251	Tale of Two Cities, A		$6.99	**$3.49**

Prestwick House

Prestwick House, Inc. • P.O. Box 658, Clayton, DE 19938
Phone (800) 932-4593 • Fax (888) 718-9333 • www.prestwickhouse.com